THE KILL JAR

Center Point
Large Print

**This Large Print Book carries the
Seal of Approval of N.A.V.H.**

THE KILL JAR

OBSESSION, DESCENT, AND A HUNT FOR DETROIT'S MOST NOTORIOUS SERIAL KILLER

J. REUBEN APPELMAN

CENTER POINT LARGE PRINT
THORNDIKE, MAINE

This Center Point Large Print edition
is published in the year 2018 by arrangement with
Gallery Books, a division of Simon & Schuster, Inc.

The text of this Large Print edition is unabridged.
In other aspects, this book may vary
from the original edition.
Printed in the United States of America
on permanent paper.
Set in 16-point Times New Roman type.

ISBN: 978-1-68324-980-1

Library of Congress Cataloging-in-Publication Data

The Library of Congress has cataloged record
under LCCN: 2018037309

For Mark Stebbins, Jill Robinson,
Kristine Mihelich, and Timothy King.

And for Dani,
for turning on a light.

*Wish I didn't know now
what I didn't know then.*
—BOB SEGER

FOREWORD

Cathy Broad

Forty years ago this past week, I gave my youngest brother, Tim, the thirty cents he'd asked to borrow so that he could walk four blocks to the store and buy candy. It had been a beautiful day, but I hesitated because it was now close to evening and Tim would have to cross a very busy road. He assured me that he would be careful, and I, seventeen years old, capitulated. Tim never returned. Six days later his body was found dumped on a roadside, one county over. Tim was the fourth victim of the entity that would become known as the "Oakland County Child Killer."

Over the decades, multiple law enforcement agencies allegedly revisited the case as leads straggled in, without resolution. I had long accepted my version of the truth: that the police had done everything they could, and that it was not uncommon for even heinous crimes to remain unsolved. Multiple writers have used the grisly and unbelievable facts of the Oakland County Child Killer case as a ready-made outline for fiction books. One nonfiction book, written back in the 1980s, was presented as a factual account, but it appears to have been written only as an effort to support the job done by the original task force investigating these crimes. The book did not dig deep.

The Oakland County Child Killer case has also been the subject of recent television shows as well as the subject of many newspaper articles that should have outraged the communities where these kids were abducted and murdered. And yet, forty years after the crimes, there are still no official answers and no official explanations of how time and money were spent investigating. There is no official resolution.

I support and applaud J. Reuben Appelman's determination to climb the very high stone walls put up by law enforcement and others who do not appear to want these crimes solved, and to give a voice to the four kids who were abducted, held captive, tortured, and murdered in one of the richest counties in America. There is so much more horror in this case than anyone could have imagined back in 1976 and 1977, and a comprehensive book on the matter has been long overdue.

Cathy Broad
Sister of Timothy King, Victim #4
March 24, 2017

INTRODUCTION

A murder scene is taped off to preserve evidence. Investigators will often return to it again and again, carefully walking through doorways, quietly standing in one corner and then another, maybe reflecting on bloodstains at the center of a room. A stain might be body-shaped and large, or it might be the size of a coin, cylindrical and small, leading to another coin-sized shape across the room, and then to another near a wall, and finally to another coin of blood that elongates now and seems to have pulled itself toward the front door, searching for exit.

Evenings are the hardest times to sleep. An investigator's bedroom is painted with the stain of cases being worked. There might also be photographs of loved ones or tastefully placed artwork on the bedroom walls, but an investigator's mind is not calmed enough by this to fall tactfully into slumber. At night beneath the sheets, a question repeats itself in the investigator's mind: How did one thing lead to another, which led to the end?

Memoir, too, is a narrative that's oftentimes best understood utilizing the techniques of a criminal investigation. To begin, a scene from one's life is taped off on the written page, preserved, and thereafter investigated. Each relevant stain in the various rooms of a memoirist's experience is revealed under lighting, sampled, and studied, until a pattern emerges. A true memoirist, restless in the evenings, snaps awake with anxiety, sometimes with dread, and eventually with awareness: How one thing led to another does, indeed, unfold in the darker hours, before illumination.

When I set out to examine an unsolved murder case, I did not yet know that my personal narrative—violent at times in its own right, even if only with longing—would collide with the narrative of the horrible crimes I'd be investigating. This story, then, became a story of the living and the dead alike. The dead and the walking are twins, after all, each the other's mirror.

During my scrutiny of the Oakland County Child Killer (OCCK) case, I meticulously mined thousands of pages of local, state, and federal case documents, including witness statements, autopsy reports, catalogues of evidence, crime scene photos, interrogation transcripts, polygraph results, and personal correspondences and interviews to assist in forming a narrative of criminal activity leading to the dead. Naturally, I also collected and studied the hundreds of local news articles written about this case over the years: They plastered my walls and imprinted my dreams. Several surviving family members of the victims were overwhelmingly generous with their time, support, and openness to being interviewed, and on occasion their stories filled in the gaps for me where official documentation could not.

But what of the gaps in the narratives of the living? Certainly, there are many private citizens, some in law enforcement, as well as my own family members, who count among the examined here. But internal lives and corresponding personal narratives are not often accounted for by documentation. One cannot simply walk into the Office of Debatable Family Matters, for instance, and file a request for the catalogue of events from Christmas morning, 1974. In time, then, I may ask myself, of the personal nuances, dialogue, and circumstances chronicled in this book, *Under whose lens were they viewed? In what moments? Under whose authority? And did I get it right?* Admittedly, I often ask myself those questions even now, for what claims to the dead or living do we truly own, be they our twins or not?

In response to that line of questioning and others, it is important to state at the outset that the OCCK crimes remain, officially, unsolved. It is my hope that the information I've gathered will assist those entrusted with the duty of resolving the many questions about these crimes that still linger. Any assumptions and opinions on my part, where they occur within the text, reflect my attempts to synthesize vast amounts of sometimes conflicting and confusing raw material into a logical narrative and do not reflect the official policy or position of any agency known to me at the writing of this book. No parties mentioned have been proven guilty of the OCCK crimes, or of association with such, in a court of law.

As the reader will find, there have been times throughout the years when both my written and internal narratives appeared to spiral uncontrollably, like Lewis Carroll's Alice, down the rabbit hole of speculation, derangement, and disorientation, although such was the condition of the hole that'd been left for me to fall through. Where I have ranged far afield, it was difficult to do otherwise and was, I hope, in service to this story, although in conflict with a more common tack.

I worry that the official and unofficial position of my family narrative will be in conflict, too. Some will undoubtedly feel betrayed by my compulsion to give new language to what had been silenced for so many years. Regrettably, I offer no great antidote to that sense of betrayal, except in stating that I betrayed myself as much as any, devolved and obsessed, and became a ghost inside my living home during the examination of what my life had amounted to. It was only in the writing that I escaped and brought to jury the evidence. It was the writing alone that allowed me to drag myself across the carpeted rooms, toward whatever we call the hoped-for light.

PROLOGUE

When I was a kid in the 1970s, a man tried to abduct me. He was about thirty-five or forty and I was seven years old, on the tail end of a stretch when multiple police departments surrounding Detroit were hunting for a kid killer.

Two boys and two girls had been murdered, each of them white, each with brown hair like mine. There were posters everywhere, with a composite sketch of a suspect, a sketch of a car—a compact, blue Gremlin with a white hockey stripe up its side—and an area of operations favoring drugstores and run-down strip malls.

They never found the guy. He'd seemingly taken kids at will, held them in his lair for many days, and then snuffed them at leisure. He was rumored to have washed their bodies with dry cleaning fluid and then set them back into the world like setting out a birthday cake full of lit candles: carefully, and with a look of accomplishment on his face.

The cops said the murders weren't about sex— they indicated to the press that none of the kids

17

had been violated that way—but about power. There was a serial abductor out there, swiping kids from their footing like sweeping a few bugs into the kill jar in his garden, and there was nothing anybody could do but keep their doors locked and ride out the storm.

The guy who tried to snatch *me* had been posing as a security guard in a drugstore. He wore a rust-colored blazer, a crisp shirt, and a dark-colored tie. He strolled along the endcaps and occasionally looked around noncommittally.

He locked eyes with me in the candy aisle while I was stuffing a pack of bubblegum into my pants pocket. I put the gum back and rushed out of the store. He followed.

I crossed a parking lot. The man got into his car.

I crossed a major intersection on foot, then tacked into my neighborhood and strolled alongside a curb where our little blue-collar houses saluted an empty street.

A minute later the man pulled up in his compact. It idled next to me, a few feet away. The passenger-side door opened and the man leaned across the center console and reached out.

I remember the details of his tiny automobile, the rattle it made, and then the creak of its door opening on a faulty hinge.

I remember the man's eyes being a greasy brown, like motor oil.

I remember the man's brown hair across the top and I remember the sideburns he wore, each crawling to the sides of his jaw.

Then my brain short-circuits, and what I begin to remember is a cigarette dangling from my father's lip on the back porch of our house in full summer, his T-shirt hugging his chest, his *Playboy* magazine draped over a five-dollar lawn chair while he did biceps curls with a barbell, twenty-five pounds on each end.

I remember my father taking my mother by her shirt and whipping her to the ground in my bedroom, and how, later that autumn, his shadow seemed long across our windows and kept my family sealed inside—nobody on the outside even knew we were there, but we did.

Somehow, the two worlds seem linked to me— the one I lived in as a young boy, and the milieu of the Oakland County Child Killer. Like planets orbiting one another, the distance eventually tightens, until they appear to collide.

Mark Stebbins, 12 years old
Dates in captivity:
Feb. 15–19, 1976

Jill Robinson, 12 years old
Dates in captivity:
Dec. 22–26, 1976

Kristine Mihelich, 10 years old
Dates in captivity:
Jan. 2–21, 1977

Timothy King, 11 years old
Dates in captivity:
March 16–22, 1977

KRISTINE

It's autumn of 2010, and I'm standing in the exact spot where ten-year-old Kristine Mihelich's ice-burned body had been found in the dead of winter, 1977. Kristine was the third victim to the OCCK, and her face, slightly plum-colored from death, had been a beacon in the freshly fallen snow off the side of this wooded residential cul-de-sac. The more slushy detritus of inner-city Detroit was thirty minutes away, but here in Franklin Village a mailman discovered Kristine on his regular route, only fifteen minutes from my own childhood home, halfway between Detroit and this old-money enclave where the trees and the bank accounts stretch equally far back.

The mailman, thirty-something Jerome Wozny, a tad homely, banked his mail truck and walked toward swaths of color off the side of the road. There'd been no blood at the drop scene, but he'd been drawn by Kristine's coat, slightly frozen to the mannequin of her torso. He stood over Kristine's body, then hurried back to his vehicle, leaving boot prints in the snow.

At the time, Franklin Village was even more wooded than it is now, pocked here and there with chimneys that ran down into great rooms, where one would find fireplaces with dogs snoring next to them, balls rolling across the hardwood flooring, the smell of bread being baked, and, more or less, families still intact between these architecturally sound walls.

Franklin Village, metaphorically, should have been hanging from a Christmas tree back then, encased in glass. When the snow fell, it seemed as if you could hear somebody moan from five houses down—it was that quiet inside the orb.

Nobody died in Franklin Village until they were old, and Kristine didn't die here, either. She'd been killed during captivity somewhere else, then driven around for a while and dumped here like a stack of newspapers hitting the curb.

Bruce Lane, the street I'm standing in and where Kristine had been tossed, bears the given name of a well-known Detroit-area psychiatrist of the time, Bruce Danto. The street wasn't named after Danto, but a lot of people immediately thought of him when Kristine's body was found, as Danto had a track record of writing about serial killers in the early seventies and a drop site with his name attached to it, even just his first name, was titillating to the local press. Conjecture was that Kristine's killer was directly challenging the psychiatrist, making a public statement with his placement of Kristine's body. Other people thought Danto himself was Kristine's murderer and that his academic fascination with serial killings was a translucent cover for the arrogant-seeming doctor with a receding hairline and bad glasses.

For a while people even suspected the ungainly mailman with only lightly developed social skills and a house full of trinkets that seemed to indicate an obsessive personality type. He'd reportedly found the body, and yet there were no other footprints in the snow besides his. Police eventually explained away the lack of what's called "impression evidence" to an overnight dithering of snowfall that would have fouled the area around Kristine's deposit, covering any tracks previous to the mailman's. A local news helicopter had further disturbed the scene, blowing snow almost immediately after Kristine was discovered, sweeping away evidence with its downdraft.

Police had interviewed the mailman after finding Kristine's body, and he'd indeed seemed "off." He was nervous, avoided eye contact, and was generally silent throughout the interview process. None of that leads to being truly suspect, of course.

He'd just found a body, was all.

"THE BABYSITTER"

Kristine had been missing for nineteen days. When the police found her and surveyed her drop-off scene, they were certain she'd been victim #3 to that entity labeled the "Oakland County Child Killer (OCCK)," also dubbed "The Babysitter" because of the way each victim had reportedly been tended to. According to investigators and the press alike, the killer had bathed his victims after death, combed their hair, clipped their nails, and even cleaned and pressed their clothes before giving them back to the world neater than when they'd gone missing: each body reportedly laid out like a new suit atop the snow, each of these suits found in various parts of the city during the thirteen months spanning from midwinter of 1976 to the end of winter in 1977.

Mark Stebbins, a twelve-year-old boy with a clean side part in his hair, was the first to go missing, snatched in daylight while walking home from his mother's work party a few blocks away. Four days later he was found dead in a parking lot. Like the sexual violence notated by the medical examiner but left out of police state-

24

ments to the press and public, evidence at the Mark Stebbins drop site was also quashed.

Jill Robinson, a twelve-year-old like Mark Stebbins, went missing ten months later. A dark-haired girl with bangs and freckles, Jill had left home with a backpack and her bicycle after arguing with her mother. The bicycle was found one day after her disappearance, abandoned behind a hobby store. Four days after Jill had been snatched, the backpack, like the bicycle, was also found, although strapped to Jill's body beside a busy freeway, a shotgun blast having disfigured Jill's face.

One week after the discovery of Jill's body, Kristine Mihelich, a ten-year-old with long, wispy hair, went missing, as well. She was found by Wozny, the mailman, nineteen days later. The time period between kidnappings had quickened, and the duration of Kristine's captivity—nineteen days versus the roughly four days of captivity for Mark and Jill—was nearly five times as long. The public obsession and hunt also quickened, and yet there'd been no reported witnesses to any of the abductions, and no reported leads.

Victim #4, Timothy King, shaggy-haired and with a wide smile and carefree eyes, was taken roughly seven and a half weeks after Kristine's body was discovered. King was found in a ditch approximately thirty minutes from home, six days after his abduction, re-dressed after having been anally assaulted and suffocated. The sexual violence associated with his killing, as with the Stebbins murder, had been left out of the official police blotter.

After the discovery of Tim's body, the story of the "Oakland County Child Killer" went into overdrive, as a witness had reportedly seen Timothy King being spoken to by an adult male standing beside a car in a parking lot just prior to King's disappearance. A composite sketch of the man, white or possibly olive-skinned, with thick, dark hair brushed backward, began to circulate in the papers, with headlines such as "Man Sought" that would soon turn into the less inspiring "No New Leads." For a period, however, with four kidnap-murders stated by police to be attributable to the OCCK, the area was swept by fear, and posters of the child killer's suspected automobile and a sketch of his face were soon Scotch-taped to every storefront and stapled to every pillar.

Hundreds of drivers were stopped on the sides of local roads for interrogation by police officers. If you drove a car resembling the one allegedly driven by the killer, getting through those few square miles of my normally user-friendly neighborhood was like trying to pass a German checkpoint during World War II. Once you got out of the suburbs and into Detroit proper, the hunt for the alleged killer was taken less seriously, but the impulse for speculation about the exact nature of his crimes loomed large, even in mostly African-American inner-city Detroit, no stranger to abduction and murder but with an interest kindled by the white-on-white, suburban opera of it all.

My own father, who resembled the abductor's composite sketch, was surrounded by police officers at a local suburban park in the winter of 1977. He'd been sitting in his car alone, during daylight, "watching the geese"—my father's euphemism for smoking pot. He was wearing a stocking cap, like a seaman's, pulled down to the tips of his ears, and his roughly cropped side-burns lined his jaw. He watched the two cruisers pull behind him, then two cops get out with guns drawn, slinking toward both sides of his car.

GETTING GONE

Before departing for Detroit from my home in Idaho, I sat and read Kristine's autopsy report in my car outside of a gas station, parked there to have privacy away from my kids and wife, to keep the darkness away from them as much as I could. The report showed Kristine to have been fed during her long captivity and then eventually asphyxiated, probably by the killer's bare hand squeezing her nose and mouth to trap the air. The murder term for this is "burking," which involves the killer restraining the victim's torso, most commonly in a bear hug, throughout the suffocation process. Burking leaves very few physical marks, if any.

I don't know what Kristine's parents thought at the time, imagining their daughter being killed in this fashion, but I can guess that the "thinking" part of them was mostly turned off. Violence just pushes against us. You don't think a goddamned thing. You just feel.

Some weeks after surveying Kristine's drop site on Bruce Lane, I went home and watched the footage I'd taken and hoped to get inside of it, but there were too many decades' distance. Where the imprint of Kristine's body had melted into the snow, flowers had sprung up, bicycles had traversed, and lawn mowers and hedgers had clipped and trimmed the grass under autumn sunlight.

KRISTINE WAS ABDUCTED on January 2, 1977, the day after New Year's Day. The first victim, Mark Stebbins, was abducted the day after Valentine's Day, 1976. The second victim, Jill Robinson, was found the day after Christmas, 1976. The fourth and presumably final victim, Timothy King, went missing shortly after Kristine was found, on the evening before St. Patrick's Day of 1977.

The dates suggest a link between holidays and the abductor's modus operandi. People have thought that, anyway, wanting to bring structure to the chaos: four dead children, four holidays. Part of being human is to pine for something linear, something we can trust that brings the pieces together like a magnet pulling back the continents to where they'd started, a logical connection like coming home, but sometimes the facts are just the facts with no narrative between them. At the time of my visit to Kristine's drop site in 2010, well over thirty years after her murder, millions of dollars and hundreds of detectives working on the largest homicide investigation in Michigan state history had failed to bring any meaningful structure to these crimes. The killer had, presumably, never been caught.

THE KILLER INSIDE

I didn't know anything about the killers out in the world in the 1970s because I was worrying about the killer inside. My family had been troubled by a darkness that hadn't yet been spoken of, but that I'd felt forming in me. The drywall in our house seemed to pulse with a sadness from the holes that'd been punched through it, when my father's right fist, sharp around the edges, like his body, would sometimes arc into the wall before he'd head out for the night.

As a child, images, oftentimes disturbing ones, stacked inside me like crudely made bricks, weighty and jagged in my mind. Killers will frequently report the same thing, being entirely driven by a single image that refuses to loosen from memory, the witnessing of a car bomb yanking a killer's grandmother into the air, or the way a broken bottle carved out his mother's ribs while he watched from a crib, transforming him while she bled out onto the cream-colored shag. No single image remade me; my transformation occurred over time, brick by brick, one thing leading to another.

When my family was running late for a party back in '76, for instance, my father threw my mother onto the floor. I don't remember why we were going to the party. We didn't often do those things. What I see now, and for all these years since, is my father wearing his suit while my mother cowers beneath him in a corner, covering herself from the threat of his lashing.

I figured he'd kill her one day, but right then all I could do was sit on the bottom bunk of my bed and stare at the television. I had a switchblade stashed in the coils above my head, just under where my brother slept, but I didn't think about using it on my father, not in that moment as protection for my mother or in any other moment—I was too afraid of him. I thought about using it on everybody else, the people outside of my family, for a lot of days afterward, and then for a lot of years, too.

I can still see the lapels of my father's 40-long suit jacket from that day. They're brown, like his wispy, goatee-style beard. My mother is on the floor, the bangs across her forehead perfectly hair sprayed, but she's oddly curled like a seahorse, the way Timothy King's body looks to me, too, decades later, in the black-and-white photo tacked to my office wall, a crime scene flashbulb lighting up the newly fallen snow surrounding his corpse.

A few months after my father whipped my

mother into the ground, I set fire to my backyard, the flames licking upward into hot daylight from a patch the size of an overturned van.

At school a few years later I threw a lit book of matches into a girl's lap for taking my queen during a chess game. I hadn't thought of her dress catching fire, before it did.

When I was a teenager, I watched pornography with another teenager I didn't know. That same year, a man washed my back in a public shower.

One time, as an adult, a stripper wrapped her legs around my waist and said, "Why don't you screw me after I get off work, then drop me back at jail."

Those images that darkened me have been compounding since childhood. Initially inherited by circumstance, I am the one who builds them now.

And brick by brick, they build me back.

THE FIRST TIME I hurt myself intentionally, I was a grown man in my mid-thirties already, probably in 2004 or 2005. I stood in the bathroom mirror and slapped myself as hard as I could with my good hand against the right side of my face. My right ear rang; it sounded like a butter knife tapping the rim of a wineglass for a toast. The slope across my jaw turned red. I did it again. The second time hurt, too, but not the way I'd expected it to.

33

That stripper on work release from the county jail had hurt me more, asked me to take off my shirt beside the stage, told me to lift my arms, spun me around while snaking out my belt. She lashed me across the back a dozen times, about ten other men in the bar watching us, some of them laughing, some of them glaring at me like I'd stolen their thunder. I'd gone home and looked at my back in the mirror, the lash marks puffy like burns. I hid my back from my wife for a week while they healed, and I felt dirty and good at the same time.

Now, it'd been a different feeling than letting a stripper inflict pain. I'd been so overwhelmed, so full to the brim with sadness from everyday life that it was the only thing I could do to come awake for a minute. My fingernails left marks when I pulled them across the swelling I'd caused, two white tracer lines dragging through a patch of red above my stubble line.

I made a fist with my right hand and when I punched myself in the cheekbone I got a bruise beneath my eye that never fully cleared up. I'd broken a blood vessel; years later, there will still be a red squiggle. I had so much pain inside that a sock to the eye had the effect of a hug somehow, an embrace from a friend who knew me well, had been there, understood my need for the pain to keep coming back to me, so that I remembered what love felt like.

At that time, I hadn't even been marked by the Oakland County Child Killer case yet. Ted Lamborgine and all of the other names surrounding the OCCK were just faded impressions out of old newspapers I'd once read.

I had no idea that in a few years I'd be pulling up their case files and beating the crap out of myself in ways that nobody could see.

Four dead kids. All of them scratched from memory and tossed into puddles like bad lottery tickets.

And everything I'd learn, and the time I'd spend learning it, would come at a price.

RICH BOY

One of the suspects in these killings, Christopher Busch, was born rich. Bearded and obese, still living in his parents' upscale home into his twenties, Busch was a child porn addict with multiple molestation charges pending against him in seemingly unrelated cases. A few weeks after being polygraphed about the OCCK murders, Busch was found dead in his home, shot through the forehead by a rifle while lying atop the sheets in the upstairs bedroom he'd spent most of his boyhood—and adulthood—in. There were no more known, related abductions after Christopher Busch's death.

The police report says that Christopher Busch's death was a suicide. The temptation is to think that he felt shame or wanted to avoid prison, that the police were on his tail and so he offed himself before the finale of being incarcerated. And yet that same report negates the presence of gunshot residue on Busch's hands, meaning it's unlikely that he fired a weapon. Additionally, four spent cartridges were found at the scene, but there was only one hole in the suspect's head.

Christopher Busch had made a good suspect but he was now a victim, too, it would seem; dirty in the case and then face-fucked with a rifle by somebody with more to lose than him.

The same police report contains no mention of blood. If you watch enough television, you know that nobody gets shot in the head without bleeding. I've held that report in my hands about a half dozen times. I keep thinking about it, waiting for the word "spatter" to appear, but it never does. Christopher Busch is a big, sheet-covered lump in the bed, reportedly bloodless, almost a ghost. A "suicide" who didn't bleed, who needed four shots to inflict one wound, who was able to fire a gun without leaving behind trace evidence.

ELLIE

It's 2010, my first night back in Detroit, a few weeks before visiting Kristine's drop site in Franklin Village. I've come only to study the case and I'm staying at a hotel off the freeway, a stone's throw from where twelve-year-old Mark Stebbins had been found. I watch TV and it's dull. The rain outside reminds me of things I don't want to think about. I get depressed watching rain.

After a while I turn off the TV and contemplate calling an old girlfriend, Ellie, whom I haven't seen in years. Ellie was the last girl I'd loved before raising kids. She was small, about five feet two inches tall, and an addict whose brown eyes turned to caramel in the right light, on summer days smoking Newports in her backyard, or when making love.

And I'd loved Ellie like a Springsteen suicide run, all heat and revved-up engines and neither of us caring that the hundred miles of freeway ahead of us might end at a brick wall, the way most people only get to love when they're young. But Ellie's addictions had made her too unpredictable, and I'd become mean inside from futilely trying to pin her down—or maybe I'd already been mean. In the end, there was just dead air between us. That was a long time ago and we've both raised kids since then, had jobs of some sort, built homes we could trust for a period.

I don't know what Ellie is like anymore but I call her anyway. She doesn't answer her phone, and I leave a message. I tell her that I'm in Detroit but I don't tell her why. I say, "I just wanted to say hi."

I hang up my phone and know I only called Ellie because I'm still dark inside. She texts me back right away.

Where are you?

I'm in a hotel, I text her.

Come over, she responds.

She texts me her address, and I stare at my phone for a while. I haven't told Ellie that my life is falling apart. I haven't told anybody this yet, and Ellie doesn't ask.

Come over. That's all.

The truth is that my marriage is in its last couple of years, maybe months. I know that my hunt for what happened to these four kids has been a part of what's destroyed us. My wife and I have tried to make it work and can't. Right now we're just riding things out until we can afford to live separately, until we can bear what the separation will do to our own kids. Fourteen years is a good run, but when I think about splitting up I still feel sad all the time. On good days I feel empty.

Even if my marriage has become a shitty one, it has offered me the warmth of pretending that I am not alone, that I have companionship in my navigation through the many bouts of depression and anxiety that have dog-eared my adulthood— and yet I know that I have been willfully clinging to a lie. My wife is less companion, more accomplice in the pretension of false love; she has spoken those words to me herself, words that are rooted like tumors inside me, have grown larger around the pain of knowing that she was right.

I text Ellie that I miss her.

I don't know what else to say and I don't even know if it's true yet, but when I think about Ellie I think of the life in me coming back. I don't think of all the times that being with her hurt. I just think of how good I felt in the moments that were good, which were like flashes of fire.

Thirty minutes later I'm standing on Ellie's tenement porch, the keys to my rented SUV gripped in my hand.

Ellie opens the door and stares at me for a moment.

Then she touches my forearm, and it's like being pulled midair across a canyon, and I don't dare look down.

LET'S START WITH THE DEAD

L et's start with the dead, but not the grouping of dead I'd expected.

The first in the photo spread, a single news article tacked to what I've been calling my "murder wall," is a female police officer. She's maybe thirty, and she's beautiful. The caption beneath her photo says, "Birmingham's first woman cop, Reni Lelek." Her black hair sweeps at the neckline, uneven bangs framing dark eyes, slightly squinted from joy at having the photo taken.

Reni Lelek has a great, so-sexy smile, showing perfect teeth, teeth that would bite you just slightly when she wanted, bite you at the chin before moving up for a kiss.

Moving across the photo spread is the former head of General Motors, Ed Cole, sixty-something and clean, in a suit-and-tie publicity shot. He's come a long way down, once gracing the cover of *Time* magazine for his role in weaning America from leaded fuel but now irrevocably underlined in this small, local paper by the caption, "Killed in a plane crash in '77."

41

And beside Ed Cole, to the right, is eleven-year-old Timothy King, whom I've come to see as my boyhood self somehow. Tim's wearing a T-shirt in the photograph, his eyes so kind they seem almost like two hands held out in offering, saying, *Have my lunch,* and *Are you okay?* At the same time, those eyes have knowledge in them, not just kindness but empathy. They're the eyes of a boy who sees pain in his forecast, even if it's subconscious. In him, I see myself at the hands of my father, and I want to hurt somebody for what none of us can change, or protect—for the broken things in our past that will never be fixed.

Beside him, eyes slanted sideways and appearing to look at Tim across the white space bordering their photos, is an art dealer named John McKinney.

McKinney is fifty-something, bearded and dark-eyed, with a light smile. I look at his photo and I don't know what I think. He seems . . . possibly like anything, which might be the point. Some people, their particular genius is in taking in, rather than giving out.

This news article, the first I'd printed when beginning my research, tells me little right now. Later, it will appear to tell me a lot.

LATE-NIGHT TV

I've been falling asleep in my hotel to HBO reruns of the movie *Couples Retreat* so I don't have to turn out the lights. I call my kids every morning and around dinnertime. I say to them "How are you doing?" And they say to me "Good." And in between my questions and their answers is a world of language gone unspoken, my longing for them to know the truth of my life, to connect with the parts of me that are broken as much as the parts that are fixed, cleaned up for display.

At night, after poring over my research, if I'm not on the phone or watching HBO, I'm thinking about Ellie.

Ellie's first boyfriend killed himself. The boyfriend after me died of an overdose. I was stuck between those two men. In a way I'm just like them, the suicide and the overdoser, my body traveling the chambers of darkened, haunted houses all the time, my fingertips dragging against the black-painted walls as I move forward in life.

It's no wonder I called Ellie.

Ellie understands what the character Dexter refers to as "my dark passenger." She's been sober for nine years, but before that it was booze and heroin and coke and whatever else was in the room. My father was doing acid, weed, coke, and booze when I was a kid, and nobody in my family went untouched by addiction into our adult lives. I'd had my first drink of red wine at the age of eleven, after a mourner's Kaddish in synagogue, and within that year I'd found a way to warm myself repeatedly from a hidden crate of alcohol in our basement, my fifth-grader's lips slugging Amaretto and rewording prayers for the dead. At dinner inside dark restaurants with my grandfather—a dapper, cuff-link–clad physician with slicked-back, thinning grey hair and a neck that smelled of Old Spice—I'd ask for the olives from his glass then suck the vodka out of them, pondering the neon bar signs and nearby prostitutes whom I could see through the restaurant windows as they loitered at corner gas stations or got into elongated cars. They reminded me of the women I'd seen in my dad's magazines, the glossy stacks of porn filling up the cardboard boxes that he'd left behind in our garage. Those magazines were full of stories whose narratives I became attached to, some of the first reading I'd done on my own as a kid. They stuck with me as a way of seeing the world through sex-colored lenses.

Later, when I began to drink on my own, I sought out those places I'd visited as a kid with my grandfather and circled them in my own car, and watched, and remembered who I was supposed to be, the man my father had taught me to craft myself into, always in the margin between death and what's before it, that space between the corners and the cars.

Somehow I have lived a lie enough to get by in the world, concealing who I am inside. And I have to continue this lie. My children are worth it.

But Ellie understands.

Ellie is like the tinted blue glow of late-night movies across my skin. I would be alone without her, abandoned to the bodies, drifting in and out of the nameless pain that has haunted me since I was a kid.

CATHY

I'm in my rented car on a side trip from Detroit to a suburb outside Chicago, five hours from my hotel. I'm holding a photocopied fourth-grade science fair award that Timothy King's older sister, Cathy Broad, had mailed to me a few months earlier. Cathy was seventeen when her brother Tim, victim #4 to the OCCK, was abducted. She'd loaned him thirty cents that evening to buy candy at a nearby store. It'd been dark out, but Tim was allowed to walk alone those few blocks through their neighborhood. The first three OCCK victims had been blue-collar, on the other side of Oakland County, whereas Birmingham, where the Kings lived with their relative wealth, still seemed untouchable, a safe place to live.

Tim never came back.

Tim's parents, whose modest two-story house was less than a mile from Christopher Busch's much larger family home, made public pleas to the abductor, on television and in the newspaper. They begged for their son, who was small for his age and mischievous. They promised Tim,

46

if he was listening, that he'd be okay. His father told Tim not to worry about the baseball tryouts he'd missed. His mother said they'd have fried chicken, his favorite meal, when he eventually returned.

Six days later Tim was found in a ditch. The papers would say he was laid out in the snow like the others had been. An autopsy report stated that his stomach contained evidence of a fried chicken dinner having been fed to him while in captivity, presumably due to his killer paying attention to Tim's mom announcing what he liked to eat.

Cathy left the Detroit area right after high school, partially to run away from the terror she'd felt in Tim's absence. She became a lawyer. She rarely talked to the press and for the first twenty-five years after his abduction played it safe and respectful with the various police departments, hoping for information to arrive.

It never did.

Now Cathy lives in a beautiful home, in a neighborhood where the streets are named after all the good presidents. There's artwork on her walls, custom cabinets, hardwood floors, signs of teenagers having trafficked through, and a spaciousness that feels helpful to getting your head right.

Cathy's smaller than I imagined her, and then I remember that Tim was small for his age, too. Like a lot of smaller, nicer people that you know, there's a bit of a knife fighter under Cathy's skin, and she's got an office full of documents on her brother's case to prove it. Over the next four hours she brings out many of those documents for review and lays them across the kitchen island. We lean in together and study her pencil markings along the margins.

Cathy looks up at some point and asks me if I know the difference between mitochondrial and nuclear DNA. I don't, even though I've spent a month reading criminal forensics books by superstars like Henry Lee and Michael Baden, both of whom worked on the O.J. Simpson case and both of whom proved Simpson guilty, although that evidence never made it into either court or the public eye because of good lawyering on the Simpson team.

"A mitochondrial DNA match," Cathy says, "would mean that your family line was matched. A nuclear DNA match would mean that you, specifically, were matched."

She tells me something about needing the bulb of the hair for a nuclear match but only a fragment of the hair for a mitochondrial match. "So," she says, "mitochondrial equals either you, one of your known relatives, or someone in your bloodline, although that could go back thousands of years. A nuclear match means, specifically, just you."

"They found a hair on Kristine fucking years

48

ago, and they never let us know," she tells me. And then she says, "They made a mitochondrial DNA match to one of Christopher Busch's friends."

Other murder cases, lots of them, have been closed based on mitochondrial DNA. I ask Cathy how she found out about the hair, the match, about all of it, and she tells me that one of the cops let her in on it. She tells me his name, says he's on TV a lot.

A year after my visit to Cathy in 2010, the mitochondrial DNA finding is leaked and the press begins writing about it. The man on the scalp end of that hair, James Vincent Gunnels, will get a lot of attention thrown his way. At first, he's in prison on other charges and can't be publicly questioned. Later, local reporters try to ambush him outside of the halfway house he moves to. Nothing will immediately come of it. The press will appear exploitative, and the man will be struggling to keep a job under the scrutiny of public accusation and drug addiction.

He'd been a teenager when hanging around with Christopher Busch, when the hair from his head was somehow transferred to Kristine's coat. He'd been fifteen and gangly, just a boy.

Now, decades later, he'd returned from prison as a man.

VINCENT GUNNELS

Mark Stebbins, victim #1, was killed in February of 1976. Kristine Mihelich, victim #3, was killed in January of 1977.

In between those dates, on May 7, 1976, Christopher Busch—the suicide victim who mysteriously didn't have any gunshot residue on his hands and, until his death, had been a prime suspect in the OCCK case—engaged in the sexual violation of the teenaged Vincent Gunnels, whom he'd been grooming for many months prior to any of the OCCK killings. Busch would later be charged with criminal sexual conduct for the Gunnels offense, while Gunnels himself would spend his adulthood in and out of incarceration.

If the mitochondrial DNA evidence is to be believed, the hair found on Kristine Mihelich belonged to either Vincent Gunnels or somebody in his family line.

When recently placed back into custody and questioned about the mitochondrial match to his hair, Gunnels told police that he was often in Christopher Busch's vehicle. That's all he would say, but in doing so he avoided directly implicating himself in the murder of Kristine Mihelich while simultaneously giving up Christopher Busch as a possibly guilty party.

He didn't say, "I don't know how that hair got on the dead girl's body."

Spending time in Busch's vehicle would account for transference of Gunnels's hair to Kristine's shirt or coat, even without Gunnels's presence during the crime itself. But it's also possible that Vincent Gunnels carried Kristine Mihelich's body and plunked her in the snow on Bruce Lane that day, transferring the evidentiary hair while doing so.

What's important is that the hair found on Kristine likely came either directly from Vincent Gunnels or from his relationship, in some fashion, to Christopher Busch's vehicle, and therefore Christopher Busch.

When I look at photos of Vincent Gunnels online—his hair cropped short, a thick mustache, his skin having whitened from spending more years under prison halogens than sunlight—I still see the boy he must have been decades prior. Cathy Broad and I talk on the phone about him throughout the next few months, speculating about his involvement with Busch, but I'm always imagining the wind in his hair and the sound of traffic as he runs across a suburban street, just being a kid, before Christopher Busch, before Kristine Mihelich, before whatever happened happened.

WELCOME TO THE CASS

Cass Corridor in the 1970s was one of the poorest areas in the country, teeming with prostitutes and junkies and welfare babies who either crawled around in the grass out front of scrap-lot homes or lined the arm's-width interior hallways of tenement housing. The streets of the Cass were isolated and potholed, with steam that rose in wintertime from iron manhole covers. Commercial buildings and homes alike were rapidly decomposing, made of brick or cinder block that peeled away in chunks and fell to the neglected streets.

Liquor stores and makeshift bars rounded out the corners of every block. Pimps surveyed their periphery, sauntering back and forth beneath lottery signs in sore need of bulb replacement.

Inside the decaying tenements, like in most ghettos, drugs were sold, weapons were exchanged, and young girls were prostituted behind bolted doors. It was the same inside the structurally unsound single-family homes that lined these short residential blocks. Most were rentals in great disrepair. Prostitutes of all ages, wearing homemade skirts that barely concealed the bruises on their legs, hustled the sidewalks outside of their homes.

Looming over the Cass neighborhood was the two-hundred-foot-tall, Gothic-looking, stone-built Masonic Temple, constructed to last for centuries. The largest Masonic temple in the world, its interior was crafted for spectacle and austerity both. A fifteen-hundred-seat, fifty-foot-high cathedral as its centerpiece loomed as large here as the Sistine Chapel does in the Vatican.

The Masonic, as it is called, contained—and still does—three different ballrooms, each of them over 17,000 square feet, as well as a 4,500-seat theater of red velvet, gold inlay, and artisan plaster to host the many symphonies, operas, and social balls underwritten by old, improbable, unthinkable money to the people of the Cass. The splendor of the Masonic amid the impoverished landscape of the Cass might seem an unlikely, even obnoxious contrast, but land in the hood is cheap, and the rich like cheap more than tact.

The Masonic's cornerstone was cemented in 1922, reportedly by the same trowel George Washington had used to mud the cornerstone on the Capitol Building in Washington, D.C. A lot happens over time, though. In the 1970s, prostitutes and their johns fucked against the building as a matter of course, the old grandeur of the Masonic encroached upon by gritty realism.

Not far from the Masonic's ballrooms and event spaces were the Brewster-Douglass Housing Projects, where Diana Ross and Smokey Robinson had grown up. The projects were five blocks long, squeezed with fourteen-story high-rises, and home to over 10,000 of Detroit's most impoverished citizens. At the time of my visit in 2010, the half-mile-long ghetto was primarily vacant, the windows boarded up or broken out. There were no plans for demolition of the massive buildings: Whatever impoverished ghosts remained, they now crackled and dragged through the halls.

In the 1970s, though, on weekend nights, suburbanites in their slicked-over sedans venturing into the Cass for an engagement at the Masonic would sometimes get lost and end up on the Eastside. I'd heard stories growing up of the terror one's grandparents had felt pulling a U-turn near the Brewster buildings.

The late '70s in Detroit saw the first seeds of carjacking sprout. People who were "fucking high as shit," as my dad would say, would skip out from the shadows with a handgun, crack it against the window to shatter it if the door was locked, and pull the vehicle's goose-necked driver through the glass.

But there were even more insidious elements than the addicts, dealers, and turf sharks at work. Running smooth as a mill in the heart of Cass Corridor was an industry of pedophilia. Hundreds of children over the course of the decade were either lured with cash offerings or "trunked," the street term for being lifted from the curb outside one's home and thrown into a car.

Scores were held in captivity, often close to home, and sold off as either feed for a blossoming child porn industry making its way underground to the East Coast hubs, or as one-offs to johns who would venture in from the suburbs during daylight for a baggie of heroin and a quickie. There were independent operators—there will always be those—but there were more profitable kid runners as well whose proficiency at the trade, and power, allowed them a measure of immunity over time.

The Detroit Police Department, presumably in order to get a grip on the Cass's rampant problem, "turned" a known pedophile of the time named Richard Lawson and employed him as a confidential informant.

Lawson, hovering at almost six and a half feet and well over two hundred pounds, occasionally gave up the odd john here and there. More often than not, though, Lawson used the police badge he had been granted by the PD—for "eventualities" related to being an informant—in much the same way the Pied Piper of lore lured children away from their village by the sound of his flute. He'd flip open his badge and the doe-eyed would follow.

Later, Lawson would be tied to one Ted Lamborgine, a sort of rock star in the pederast scene in Pontiac thirty miles outside Detroit.

Ted Lamborgine will begin to come up more in my research and will eventually be tied to Christopher Busch through the testimony of one of Busch's molestation victims, a boy who survived his rape by Busch but who will claim to have crossed paths with victim #4, Timothy King, during King's captivity.

THE SCHVITZ

The Schvitz is a steam house a few blocks from Cass Corridor central and the Masonic. A relic from the 1930s, the Schvitz is built like a warehouse: made of concrete, nondescript, twenty feet high and about fifty feet long, with no windows and a single unmarked door.

Weeds growing up its side, the Schvitz is the type of place you could disappear inside of. Most buildings in Detroit are like this, vacant-seeming even if they're not, the exteriors unpainted for decades, crumbling with decay. But to me the Schvitz exterior presents an intentional illusion; it's *supposed* to look dumpy. Goings-on happened here, and, I am told, continue to happen here, that specifically require a lack of notice from passersby.

Around its inception, members of the Purple Gang, known as the Jewish Mafia, took saunas at the Schvitz, ate steak dinners, and got smacked on the back with soaped-up mops of grape leaves. Years after that, the Schvitz became more illicit: In the1960s, homosexuals could mingle there in privacy, have furtive sexual encounters in the dimly lit rooms, and then go home to their wives and day jobs.

By 1985, when I was fifteen, the same age Gunnels had been while riding in Christopher Busch's car, I'd had my own dark suitor, a man in his mid-forties who'd been grooming me, only I was too young to know what that meant. The father of a friend, he'd taken me and a couple of other boys to the Schvitz for an afternoon steam.

Like any father of any friend, I'd thought, only slightly sharper. He used to kiss me on the cheeks when he said hello, first one side of my face and then the other—like mobsters, or like the Europeans—and I'd smell the pomade in his slicked-back hair and the aftershave on his face when he leaned in.

On weekends, he'd come into the bagel store where I worked my first job, and he'd bullshit with whatever boy was there but especially with me, it seemed, always leaning over the counter to touch faces, sometimes grabbing the back of my head to bring us closer. I just went along with it. He was nice, he wore expensive jewelry that impressed me, and I didn't want to disappoint him by being cold. I didn't find him threatening at all. Later, he invited me to the bathhouse with two of the other boys.

Without asking permission from my parents, I went, and although those other boys went along with us, his attention seemed focused on me while we all undressed in a locker room and wrapped clean white towels around our waists for the short walk to an indoor hot tub. We soaked in silence for a while, the man leaning his head back against the rim of the tub and relaxing. When we got bored, we stepped out of the tub and dripped across ancient-seeming tiles to a steam room, the three of us boys wearing thin, inexpensive gold chains that glistened with sweat and heat against our undeveloped chests. The man wore his own gold chain, thick like a rope.

We sat in the steam room for a while, the hot, mentholated air filling my lungs, then retired to a dining room, still wearing only our towels, which seemed odd to me.

In the dining room were several cloth-covered tables but no other patrons, as if the room had been reserved just for us.

We were served a steak-and-salad meal. It was long past lunchtime but not quite dinnertime yet. I had never eaten a meal practically naked before, but I liked it. I felt like I was in a Mafia movie.

Done eating, we pushed our plates aside, and the man said, "We'll see a movie now."

He stood up and we followed him to a small viewing room with a heavy door that he opened for us. I could see inside the room to a series of large leather recliners facing a sedan-sized movie screen. The man put his arm around my shoulder as I went in.

"If you have to do anything in there," he said, "just do it, you know?" I wasn't sure of what he was talking about, but I figured it out soon enough.

I sat in a recliner and the man sat in a recliner nearby. The door shut behind us and the room went fully dark. After a few awkward moments a porn film started rolling from a projector at the back of the room.

I watched the movie and felt anxious. Two people screwed onscreen, some other people screwed onscreen, and then at some point the movie was over and the lights in the room slowly ascended. We stood up in our towels and exited the makeshift theater.

Naked and soapy in the shared showers while we rinsed off afterward, the man stepped too close to me and rubbed his hands over my back. "Let me get that for you," he said, pretending that the two feet of spine moving down from my neck was something that needed procedural attention, his ringed, heavy-feeling fingers landing between my shoulder blades before I could turn away.

The first touch, for a predator, must be exhilarating. For me, as his prey, the first touch was paralytic.

I GOOGLE THE address for the Schvitz, then put it into my GPS and steer through side streets. When I get out of my SUV, I step around a massive pothole full of water and motor oil. There's no traffic. I stand in the street and recognize nothing, but there's a small handwritten sign on a stick in the ground that reads SCHVITZ PARKING and then an arrow pointing around back. Without that handwritten sign I wouldn't know I was here, and I presume that's exactly the point.

The houses up the street are partially boarded, most of them written off as abandoned. Squatters have taken over. Adorning the nearby porches are half-fixed children's bicycles, makeshift laundry lines of electrical wire, and the occasional gas station–issue hibachi. There's a man sitting on a concrete stoop fifty yards away, staring at me.

When I walk to the back of the building, I think about Timothy King and the route he'd taken in Birmingham to get home. He'd left a pharmacy through the back door at night, crossed a poorly lit parking lot, and never gotten to finish his five-minute walk home. Somebody stuffed him into an automobile, we can presume. The details of the precise moment of abduction are not known to the public or to me. What is known is that things happen to us within eyeshot of the rest of the world and nobody recognizes it as a "happening" until it's done. Ellie's ex-boyfriend, for instance, hung himself in a closet with his own belt, by lifting his legs off the ground. I believe his parents found him hanging like that, but in the dead space between the act and the discovery of the act there was no recognition from the world, no gesture of understanding that a man was looping a leather belt around his neck for impractical purposes. Outside my high school once, I saw a kid sitting by himself and thought he was a loser. Two days later there was an announcement over the PA that he'd shot himself. We had a moment of silence. When I was nine, a boy pushed me on the playground and I actively hated him for it. That year his whole family died of carbon monoxide poisoning while they slept.

I want to believe that in the lead-up to death there are signs, but there usually are not.

HERE'S THE MOST beautiful feeling I have ever had: It's probably the same as yours, but I was drunk when it happened. I just want to be better than that now. I want to feel joy but the only way I know how to is to feel the darkness beforehand. I have to fuck myself up in order to call myself a survivor.

In the back of my mind is always the memory of my father punching my brother so hard it left dots on his back from the meshing of his little Detroit Lions jersey—or the memory of weed smoke on my brother's friends when they were eleven and I was six, and how my brother used to hide his pot in a hollowed-out Foreigner eight-track.

Or the glass bullets of cocaine I'd found in a

wicker basket my dad kept, or how my sister used to sit in her bedroom all the time and just cry for what seemed like no reason.

Or the stacks of *Hustler* magazine in our garage and how I burned down our backyard looking at one of the centerfolds and playing with matches at the same time—how sex and fire mingled.

THERE WAS SOMETHING about my darkness that Ellie completely understood. No matter what I was doing, Ellie had already done worse, lived through worse, felt worse about herself. But our relationship was cosmic, too, if you believe in that shit. I always felt my skin vibrating in her presence, even when she'd done something hurtful.

The best thing about being with Ellie was never having to hide, never needing a bar or a warehouse to conceal my sins. I could hold Ellie and cry to her and know she was there. I could fall to pieces and still get up feeling like a man.

You don't get that feeling walking out of the Schvitz.

You want to smoke a cigarette, get robbed in the parking lot, stick a knife into somebody. You want to drive your car into the river and drown.

But none of that happens.

You walk out of the Schvitz and you go home, and that's sometimes worse than anything violent. There's a huge mega-freeway of ache inside you, and it's empty, and you're the only one on it.

And nobody even knows it's there besides you. And if you tell anybody, your whole life is over in a blink. And so you don't.

Whoever killed these kids had that feeling inside. I know it. The cops will argue differently, that psychotics don't feel, but my hunch tells me to follow the loss.

JILL ROBINSON

Twelve-year-old Jill Robinson had left home on her bicycle three days before Christmas after an argument with her mother. She was wearing a small backpack and was thought to have been in transit to her father's home in a nearby suburb. She was found four days later on the side of busy Interstate 75, which connects the Detroit area to wooded northern Michigan hundreds of miles away, still wearing her back-pack but with part of her head broken away from a shotgun blast.

Jill had been dropped in the snow at night, only a half mile from an on-ramp beside the Troy Police Department, twenty-five minutes from Detroit proper. A witness later described a blue Pontiac LeMans pulled to the shoulder at four thirty a.m. The LeMans will come up again at the Kristine Mihelich site, based on a rear bumper imprint in the snow, but nobody ever talked about the LeMans in the early dissections of the case. The only vehicle of interest anybody in the police ever talked about, and released information about to the press, was a blue AMC Gremlin, based on uncorroborated eyewitness testimony from the Timothy King abduction site.

Regardless of physical evidence supporting the LeMans as a lead, it was buried, and throughout nearly all of my early research the blue Gremlin is still the only vehicle that shows up online, is talked about by friends or publicized in old radio shows and news video as the vehicle of interest. When asked about the Oakland County Child Killer of lore, nearly everybody who grew up in Oakland County at that time remembers the Gremlin—nobody speaks of a LeMans despite its appearance in the case files.

Jill Robinson's condition presented another mystery beyond the murder itself: the shotgun blast to her head. Since the other three victims were asphyxiated, it was speculated that she'd given her killer a hard time and that he'd panicked or gone into a rage, altering his MO. The pathologist listed Jill's cause of death as hemorrhage and shock from the wound, which would certainly have killed her, but a theory iterated to me by Jack Kalbfleisch, a retired original task force member living in Florida, is that Jill Robinson was asphyxiated prior to a postmortem shotgun blast.

"She was placed inside the LeMans," the ex-cop Kalbfleisch tells me during our two-and-a-half-hour phone call. I'd been in my car out by the mall in Troy and pulled into a parking lot to talk to him. His voice sounds old now but he'd barely been out of cop school when the crimes went down. "Then she was taken to her drop site," he says, and speculates that Jill was hoisted onto the shoulder of somebody who carried her into the snow. The guy held a shotgun in his free hand as a defense against any interruptions in the drop. When he plopped Jill onto her final resting spot, the backpack she'd been dressed in forced the remaining air out of her lungs, causing a moaning sound to expel through the vocal cords.

Kalbfleisch adds, "Whoever carried her out there would have thought she was still alive, pointed the shotgun at her head, and squeezed off a round of buckshot." He says that dead bodies often expel air, and noise. It would account for the killer changing his MO.

One set of footprints was left in the snow. What may also have been left in that moment was trace evidence on the torso section of Jill Robinson's coat. Like the hair found on Kristine, hairs from the shooter's head may have rubbed off while carrying Jill, although nothing in my research has, so far, shown that to be the case. What we might assume about the shotgun that blasted Jill Robinson in the face was that it was double-barreled, because twelve-year-old Mark Stebbins, victim #1, was found to have suffered a blow to the head that left two circular side-by-side imprints. There were two dead-together zeros stamped into his skull as if the barrel of the shotgun had jabbed his skin—somebody shoving the gun against his head to entice him to walk forward, maybe. When found on his corpse, the wound showed signs of healing, meaning it had been inflicted days before his murder, which, like the rest of the murders, was performed by suffocation.

All I can know with certainty about the Jill Robinson drop site is the method of carrying her into the snowbank. Based on a single set of footprints and the positioning of her body, the carrier, who was also the presumed killer, held Jill Robinson over his right shoulder—the way he must have carried Kristine Mihelich, too, based on her positioning in the snow at the end of Bruce Lane.

The killer was right-handed, using his stronger arm to lift and balance the bodies before delivering them. And he didn't have to be particularly strong to do so. These were children the killer was toting. They weighed practically nothing. And here's how a guy lifts you when you're nothing: He just fucking lifts you.

THE INTERNET SLEUTH
AND HER SUSPECT

Inside the American Legion Hall party that twelve-year-old Mark Stebbins had departed minutes before his abduction on February 15, 1976, a twenty-something man named John, dark-haired and thin, in attendance at his mother's work party, had been mingling with guests before leaving hastily. Some say he left to go after the Stebbins boy.

John and Christopher Busch, contemporaries in age, lived in the same upscale neighborhood in Bloomfield, just a few blocks away from one another, which I learn from checking their 1976 addresses on my phone. Although Busch appeared to have no hobbies outside of pornography, John, according to statements his relatives had given to the police, came to grips with the world around him through drawing, mostly in pencils and common ink. He was good at it and, in 1976, had recently returned from Europe, where he'd briefly studied art—now he was bumming around Detroit without direction.

John's father was an executive in the automotive industry. He provided well enough for his family that they were able to afford the price tag of a home in Bloomfield Hills, one of the five wealthiest suburbs in the United States at that time. It was a relatively close-knit community. Christopher Busch and John, being the same age, living within close proximity to one another, and each having well-off fathers with executive positions in the auto industry, would likely have crossed paths socially. Their fathers' paths would likely have crossed professionally.

In 1977, John was reported as a person of interest to the original OCCK Task Force by a tipster. He was questioned about the crimes but also about other suspects, including Christopher Busch. He claimed not to know who Busch was, even though you could fire a slingshot from John's front porch and the ball bearing would land in the Busch family yard if you put the correct arc on it.

John was crossed off as a suspect and investigators ignored him until 1992, when his name was again offered by yet another tipster, who claimed that John had confessed to the OCCK murders a year earlier. This new tipster, "Helen" Dagner—her real name, I've read online, is otherwise, but she goes by Helen in her correspondence—was a middle-aged woman who claimed that she'd met John in Alpena, a neighboring town to Ess Lake, where the Busch family had their cottage.

Dagner's husband, Wally, had been a cop in Rogers City, just north of Alpena, at the tip of the lower peninsula of Michigan and facing Lake Huron, a 23,000-square-mile freshwater body larger than the Caspian Sea. Since her husband's suicide in 1983, Helen Dagner had nurtured an obsession with the underworld, police files indicate, and had eventually turned informant to minor crimes in the area. At some point, it seems from internal police emails and memos, Dagner had a personal relationship with a local detective but appears to have lost favor with the PD for what was characterized as her obstinate behavior.

In Dagner's 1991 statement to police, she said that she'd spent time with the mother of John's young daughter, who was six then, and that Dagner had eventually developed a trusting friendship with John himself that teetered on romance but never went further. John, she said, like herself, seemed interested in discussing criminal activity, so they were drawn to one another and had lengthy intellectual conversations about darker, disquieting topics that most people shied away from.

Dagner and John saw each other frequently. At some point, according to Dagner, John told her about being interviewed by the original OCCK Task Force as a suspect in the 1976–77 killings. Dagner was immediately titillated. She and John, after this disclosure, either went to coffee or met at his apartment nearly every evening for a year. John seemed to know an endless amount of information about the case, and Dagner never got enough of listening to him postulate about the killer's motives and lifestyle.

"The killer really took good care of them," she claimed that John told her. He fed the kids their favorite foods, groomed them, and was generally "real nice," probably only murdering them, he said, to save them from the misery of their coming lives. John speculated that the killer was inadequate socially, couldn't get a girlfriend, and wound up doing odd jobs "like working in restaurants." While the killer lived in a well-off community, John further speculated, his mother may have had to babysit for extra income, to make ends meet.

At first Dagner was fascinated by John's imagination, which seemed married to an intellect and single-minded ability to recall even the minutest details he'd read in the papers nearly fifteen years prior. After a while, however, Dagner began to suspect that John himself was the killer. He, too, was inadequate socially, had no current girlfriend, did odd jobs for a living, and complained that, although financially well-off, his father had sequestered their wealth and forced the family to live a meager existence.

Dagner told police that she pressed him for more "theories," feigning attraction, intuiting a potential confession from the man. Over time, she reported, John began to divulge even more about the OCCK crimes. He drew Dagner maps of the drop sites and routes the killer might have driven. He revealed details of the clothing the children wore and what items they'd had in their possession when abducted. Dagner would check what John had told her against old news articles and came to believe that some of the things he'd said had never been printed in the papers. John was either lying or had intimate knowledge of the case, it seemed. His storytelling was so specific and relentless that she felt it had to be the latter.

By her account, John finally confessed to Helen Dagner over coffee at the Big Boy restaurant in Alpena sometime around Christmas of 1991. She called the Alpena police, the Birmingham police, and several family members of the victims within weeks of his confession, all in early 1992, reporting the details of their conversations. Much of what she reported they'd talked about, both intimate and unpublished, turned out to be factual.

When she first went to the Birmingham police, they reminded her that the original task force had written off John because he'd had a passport showing he'd not yet returned from Europe at the time of the Stebbins murder, but Dagner claimed that John had laughed at their incompetence, stating that, in fact, he'd owned two passports, one a fake that he'd shown to the cops to avoid further scrutiny.

She continued to tell the police more than they'd likely expected from her. She reminded the police that all four OCCK victims were abducted or dropped off on Sundays and Wednesdays and that John, employed as a cook, had these days off from work. She pointed out to the PD that John matched the original composite drawing, which was of interest but just as circumstantial.

She reported that John had told her that a different car was used for each abduction; although one of the automobiles had indeed been a Gremlin, it wasn't blue.

The children, John had said, were given manicures during captivity. Dagner told police that while in John's home she'd discovered a professional-grade mani-pedi set purposefully concealed in a shoe box behind a drawer in a normally locked office. The children had all been abducted during snowfall in winter months, and Dagner reported that John would go into an eerie mental state while watching the snow and that he'd become completely unaware of others in his presence or of words being spoken to him.

None of this was very important to the police. Lots of people became contemplative, even depressed and isolated mentally, during snowfall. How many people in the universe had Sundays and Wednesdays off? Things weren't immediately adding up—until Dagner told them that, at some point in their discussions, she'd slyly asked John where he'd purchased the fried chicken that Timothy King was found to have eaten, and John had replied, "I cooked the chicken."

Realizing he'd confessed, Dagner said, John reportedly then let the floodgates open. He'd told Dagner that Jill Robinson's backpack contained a compact, cosmetics, and a blanket, and that nothing was missing when he dropped her off. He'd said that his father owned two houses, the one the family lived in and the one next door, a rental that was often vacant, where John had held the children for brief periods. Dagner claimed that John alluded to the existence of Polaroid pictures of the crimes. She said that he'd drugged the kids with "a sleeping drug" before suffocating them.

In addition to many hours of police testimony divulging their conversations, Dagner gave circumstantial evidence that might implicate John in pedophilia, other sexually illicit activity, or generalized sexual dysfunction, which did not prove John a killer but appeared, to the police, to add greater merit to a fuller investigation of the man. She said that John, in addition to the books he collected on fingerprinting analysis, forensics, and polygraphs, surreptitiously owned a tourism book called *A Guide to Nude Beaches* and the pages where children appeared naked were dog-eared.

John's ex-girlfriend, who'd given birth to his daughter, was interviewed in 1992. She concurred with some of Dagner's allusions, telling investigators she thought John "was a pervert." While breastfeeding their baby once, she'd discovered John watching from behind a curtain, masturbating, she'd said. She'd once found women's underwear and a vibrator wrapped tightly in plastic, she said, tucked into a bag he kept hidden. Again, although circumstantial, her statements corroborated the impression of John as someone whose sexual appetites were considered by police to be outside the norm of that time. She and John were only romantic for a short period, she'd said, between 1986 and 1987. John would stay for a couple of months, then disappear for a couple of months before eventually returning. She didn't know where John stayed during those periods away from her.

Another ex-girlfriend, from his days in Birmingham, was subsequently interviewed and told the police that John used to fold her arms across her chest and hold them tightly while they had sex. She'd thought he was privately into bondage but just wouldn't talk about it. The crossing of her arms was of interest to the PD because of the way in which the OCCK's victims had possibly been burked. Today it's hard to imagine that any sexual fetish indulged by consenting adults would draw attention, but in an era predating wide exposure to Internet porn, John stood out to the cops.

John's mother was also questioned in 1992 and described her son as a loner but also as a natural-born artist. The rough dates she provided for his trip to Europe implied the possibility that John and Busch had crossed paths overseas, their two dates of travel overlapping. During her statement to the police, John's mother veered from direct questioning, at first telling of circumstances where her son was beaten by black men at a temporary job he'd had with General Motors, then ranting about a plot by the Japanese to take over American economic policy. She stated that her son performed backbreaking work at GM while "black workers sat and watched." From the perspective of the police, the statements she'd provided to them were of questionable merit and absent of leads.

Sometime in 1992, not having been charged in any capacity, John moved to Atlanta, Georgia, where a little over a decade earlier the abduction-homicides known as the Atlanta Child Murders had occurred, from 1979 to 1981, relatively soon after the OCCK murders ended—a notation of coincidence, not consequence.

Police records show Dagner corresponded with multiple law enforcement personnel about the case for over twenty years. She once ran a personal website containing thousands of posts about the OCCK murders but pulled it down. While a lot of Dagner's claims about John have had fist-sized holes punched through them, certain early details about the case, which only insiders should have had knowledge of, appear accurate.

Dagner's husband, Wally, committed suicide on November 20, 1983. After Dagner told John about her husband's death in one of their early conversations, John reportedly commented to her, "That's odd. I knew somebody who committed suicide on that same day, five years prior."

Dagner mentioned this to detectives in 1992. She didn't know that her husband's suicide and the "suicide" that John mentioned had any more weight to it than the incidental. The detectives thought differently. They checked their records and confirmed that John had likely been talking about Christopher Busch's suicide, not yet public in reference to the OCCK murders.

On November 20, 1978, exactly five years earlier to the day that Helen Dagner's husband, a Rogers City police officer, had reportedly killed himself with a gunshot wound to the chest, Christopher Busch was found shot in the head by a gun that left no residue on his hands.

THE ALPENA WITNESS

Over the years, OCCK investigators have apparently found enough merit in the John lead to repeatedly investigate him. In 2008, Michigan state detectives traveled to Atlanta, Georgia, questioned John, and took a DNA swab from inside his cheek to compare against evidence. No match was found.

In August of 2009, police again went to Atlanta and met with John in a vehicle in an empty parking lot at the Church of the Apostles, on Northside Parkway. I've read their report, and the transcript of the interview, conducted by Detective Sergeant Garry Gray of the Michigan State Police and Detective Cory Williams of the Livonia PD.

John had sat in the back of an unmarked police cruiser. Physically ailing and no longer in touch with his daughter, who was twenty-two by then, he appeared a bit jumpy to the police. He denied ever knowing Christopher Busch and claimed to have spoken with Helen Dagner on only one occasion about the OCCK killings—at the Alpena Big Boy, as she'd claimed—but John said they'd spoken only in a cursory way about the murders. He stated that he'd made no suggestion to Dagner that he had private information or that he'd been involved in the murders. He claimed that Dagner had a vendetta against him, due to her unrequited romantic urges.

What John didn't yet know is that, in 2006, someone claiming to be a witness to his conversation with Dagner at the Alpena Big Boy in 1991 had contacted the police and supported Helen Dagner's story. The Alpena witness, a middle-of-the-road conservative employed as an engineer and with no police record, stated that he'd been browsing the Web for information about another infamous murder case, that of the much-studied BTK killings. He'd stumbled onto Helen Dagner's website through a link devoted to serial killers.

When he read Dagner's blog entries about the Alpena Big Boy, he told police, his blood froze. He remembered the odd night he'd spent in the Big Boy restaurant listening to that strange man, now known to him as John, seemingly confess to a series of child murders. What he'd heard was so bizarre that he'd simply passed it off as a hoax. He'd even partially doubted his own ears, but when he read Dagner's description of the John conversations on her website he knew he'd overheard what seemed to be a true confession fifteen years earlier.

The witness had been sitting one booth behind Dagner and John on December 26, 1991. When he first sat down, he could tell the two intimates were deep in discussion. Place mats were spread around their table and Dagner and John leaned in toward one another. He heard John speak the words "drop off" and "murder." He leaned over slightly and watched as John roughly penciled out street locations on a few place mats. The maps seemed to highlight different routes along Interstate 75 from Detroit to Flint and within northern Michigan.

The witness thought that John must have been a cop but then he distinctly heard John say, "I wanted to live with the children before I killed them." He said it sounded like John was trying to impress Dagner. At the same time, the way John talked was more urgent, "like a lid was blown off," as he told police in his statement.

When John started talking about giving the children baths, the witness got skeptical. They were in a public place, and John was speaking too freely for it not to have been a joke. Still, the witness was fascinated with the story. John seemed to tell it spontaneously, pulling a wealth of information from memory. His tone when speaking about the now-dead children was like that of someone speaking of a dear friend. The witness heard John say they'd watched television together and played games, and that John had prepared dinners for the kids.

Darkly, John described sticking something up the rectum of one of the boys after killing him. One of the girls, he said, had enjoyed the song "Lucy in the Sky with Diamonds" by the Beatles. John used hand gestures to imitate how he had "shot her in the head in the snow."

The witness was visiting Alpena on vacation with his wife and two children at the time of his eavesdropping. He left the Big Boy to meet up with his family, who had been waiting for him back at the Holiday Inn, he told the police. The cops checked the hotel records and verified his stay at the hotel. They found the Alpena witness to be credible, but once again there was no hard evidence to base an arrest on.

When the police took a cheek swab from John in 2008, they didn't tell him about the Alpena witness from two years earlier, but in 2009, in the church parking lot, they spoke to him at length about it. Detective Williams stated that he had spoken to the Alpena witness once again in May of the current year, and affirmed, he told John, that the witness "is an independent person" who corroborated Dagner's story of the alleged confession by John in the Alpena Big Boy. The detective told John, "He has a good job, is married, has kids, [and has] nothing to do with Helen Dagner."

John remained firm in his denial of the statements that Dagner, and now another, had attributed to him. And he appears to have satisfied the investigators that he was not involved.

THE RABBIT HOLE

I'm taking the John C. Lodge Freeway into central Detroit, back to Cass Corridor. It's raining again, just after sunup, and there's a stream of taillights in front of me as I dodge the car-sized potholes toward downtown.

I'm thinking about the drugs that might have been used by the killer to keep his victims sedated. Tim's sister, Cathy, had told me that Tim's toxicology report negated the presence of ethanol, barbiturates, carbon monoxide, pain relievers, halocarbons (toxins used in fertilizer and dry-cleaning solution), Quaaludes, psychotic tranquilizers, opiates, Valium, and sleeping pills.

I pick up my cell and call a doctor friend I've known since grade school. He tells me about a drug called suxamethonium chloride. It's crystalline, white, and odorless. It enjoys the fastest onset and shortest duration of all known muscle relaxants. It doesn't last long but does get into the bloodstream quickly. When absorbed, an animal or human is temporarily paralyzed but fully aware, conscious of events but unable to prevent them from happening.

The drug is most often used in veterinary clinics to induce this short-term paralysis before euthanizing large animals. I learn later, through happenstance, that John worked at a veterinary clinic in the years prior to the OCCK killings.

The information I gain working on the case sometimes doesn't add clarity but, rather, when I run it down, muddles what otherwise might be a lucid-seeming narrative. There's just too much to think about, the hundreds of newspaper articles spilling out of Bankers Boxes in my hotel room in Detroit, as well as back home in Idaho; the reels of microfilm swishing right to left in the many libraries I visit in the suburbs here; the sheaths of interview transcription stacked atop my bed-sheets, their language betraying good and bad cops, good and bad suspects, truth and something murkier. When I add the information I get just talking to people, in person or online, I get even more lost.

This feeling of getting lost has lately been masked by a newer, more false sensation, seem-ingly spontaneous with each fresh source, of getting close. When you receive new information, the eyes open wide, flooded with adrenaline. You move fast toward something but you don't know what it is yet. Everyone on any hunt does, but it's like frantically swimming toward a buoy to save yourself when you'd left dry land on purpose.

There's a guy, for instance, who people online

say killed somebody in the 1960s. I spent hours one night reading about him, getting sidetracked. His name was Stephen Stanislaw, and his uncle was a state representative at the time. Stanislaw reportedly used an aviation rope in his killings. He was an avid flyer, as was his father, a former Michigan aeronautics commissioner. Coincidentally, Stanislaw's old man knew JonBenét Ramsey's old man through aeronautics circles, although they weren't contemporaries. JonBenét is one of this country's most famous murdered children, her case unsolved after more than two decades, just another of so many kids murdered without resolution to the mystery of how it happened.

According to online reports, Stanislaw did no time on the suspected murder case from the 1960s. Already known to police, he was later questioned about the OCCK killings, but his family provided alibis. Later he murdered his father, one of the alibi providers. He went to a mental facility for fifteen years, I read, from 1981 to 1996. (In another notation of coincidence, not consequence, two weeks after Stanislaw's release, JonBenét was killed.)

The more you dig, the more you see danger around every corner. If I'm not careful, each new piece of information will indeed lead to another, so far forward that I will have surpassed the truth. Did Stanislaw have anything to do with the

OCCK crimes? It's highly doubtful, but if I'm not careful I will start to believe in a connection. It's what happens to people who travel this road, who fall through the hole, this connecting of the darkest dots ad infinitum, until we're tumbling and disoriented, while the rest of the world, living above us, remains deaf to the suction.

THE ART DEALER

In Detroit, it's hard not to see a connection between poverty and politics. Reports of government corruption make the news every year like clockwork. The city's first black mayor, Coleman Young, served for twenty years, from 1974 to 1994, and, while initially applauded among the black community, spent his two decades instating cronies to fill a personal coffer rivaling old money. He ruled the city limits with a freshly minted fist; trolled for allies in the church, the police, and the courts; doled out bribes and gifted millions in no-bid contracts. He held on to his power in third-world fashion, strong-arming it from the people.

During Young's tenure, a drug cartel known as Young Boys Inc.—the name is only coincidental to the mayor's name—seeing huge pockets of heroin use in the city, consolidated the independent drug dealers and eventually controlled all of the heroin traffic in Detroit. It was estimated that Young Boys pulled in $750,000 a day. They had a street reputation for creative vendetta tortures that included sharpened broomsticks and alligators in sealed basements. Where so much heroin saturated the city, there was an equal spike in prostitution and violent crimes.

The mayor did little to curb the violence until the late 1980s, when soon-to-be police chief Ike McKinnon spearheaded a major raid on Young Boys, arresting sixty of its lieutenants. Prior to that, in the 1970s, Ike McKinnon headed the sex crimes unit in Detroit. Among his territories was the impoverished Cass Corridor and the unlit corners in the environs of the Masonic.

According to McKinnon, the pedophile turned informant Richard Lawson was paid in cash by the Detroit PD for his particular knowledge of pedophilia within the city and its environs. In exchange for the badge they'd given him to get out of trouble with, Lawson steered the city's sex crimes unit toward multiple arrests over the years, although they were of lesser consequence than the damage Lawson did himself, his exploits in the underground unknown to the public until 2006, when he went up for the 1989 murder of a cab company owner.

During testimony in his murder trial, Lawson bragged about his ties with police in the 1970s. He gave up Ted Lamborgine as being connected to the OCCK and recounted stories about Cass Corridor and Cass Community United Methodist Church, whose pastor, Reverend Lewis Redmond, was of special interest.

The Reverend Redmond inherited a church in Cass Methodist that had spent previous decades catering to the wealthy; now, with the flight of Detroit's moneyed to its suburbs, Lewis Redmond's church was the epicenter of a broken community that was financially and spiritually impoverished. Under the reverend's vision, however, Cass Methodist began to focus almost entirely on the poorest children of the Cass. The homeless and drug-addicted, the developmentally disabled, and the homebound elderly were targeted for care.

As a community volunteer with Cass Methodist, Richard Lawson had both God and the law on his side, the church and the police, with access to the vulnerable wherever he looked. The Cass became a fourteen-block-long, four-block-deep corridor of opportunity for those with insidious motives. Lawson led the pack, impervious to consequences.

MUCH OF THE Cass's population was white in the 1970s, although no more moneyed because of it. The whites back then were those without the accumulated wealth to flee after a 1967 riot that scared the hell out of most Caucasians with a savings account. The whites left behind were the most destitute, scavengers who roamed the vacated city for trifles. They mingled in jazz clubs with their black neighbors; overdosed in barren tenements with the same needles in their arms; "sold the same pussy," as people said, on street corners; and trusted in the same system of churches and government to recognize their need.

The only time Cass Corridor saw money or power take notice, it came in the form of a "buy." Like other suburbanites who came to the Cass for an easy score, the art dealer John McKinney used to roll in from the suburbs. Sporting his blazer, he'd slink up the stairwells toward any number of well-worn mattresses. Later, he'd drive back to his residence near 15 Mile, a few dots on the map from Timothy King's family.

ONE DEGREE OF SEPARATION

The art dealer John McKinney was murdered six months after Timothy King's abduction, in 1977. McKinney sometimes spent nights at his gallery in Birmingham, Michigan. He had a disco-trim beard, a casual hairstyle, two girlfriends who would visit him at the gallery, and a wife and a home a few miles away. He was very involved in both his Christian-based church as well as in extracurricular cult activities: He was officially a reverend of a second, "hidden church," as the papers called it after his death. A reported drug user (but who wasn't, in the 1970s?), he was shot down in his art gallery one night, the case never to be officially solved. In the xeroxed photograph I have of him on my wall, McKinney's eyes peer away from the camera, looking sidelong.

According to a police source who worked his murder scene, John McKinney had shared a glass of wine with his murderer just prior to the time of death. He was beaten savagely afterward. He was then allowed to wash up and, shortly after that, killed with a .22-caliber weapon, assumed to be a pistol.

The crime started in an office located on the second floor of McKinney's gallery. The scene there indicated a struggle followed by the aforementioned beating. The bathroom where he washed his own blood away was one floor down, at street level. Close to the bathroom, near a rear exit door, McKinney was shot to death. It is unknown if he was leaving with the killer or attempting to escape when he was shot.

Nothing of great value was taken from McKinney's gallery, although he catered to high-dollar clients and there was much to abscond with if robbery was the motivation for his death sentence. The single item taken was what artists call a "soft sculpture"—in this instance, a three-by-five-foot series of ropes formed into a sort of web on the wall. Priced at $800, the rope sculpture was cheap compared to most of the pieces in McKinney's gallery.

At his funeral, according to one local news article, the pastor was overheard saying, "What we knew of John McKinney, he should be in heaven. But from what we have heard, he is probably in hell." It's safe to say that there were many parts of McKinney's life that were a secret until after his death.

In the *Birmingham Eccentric* newspaper article about the area's biggest stories of the year, Tim King and John McKinney have the side-by-side photos, John McKinney to the right. Tim looks like a sweetheart. McKinney looks like Jack Nicholson in *The Shining* but with a little more hair. The two photos, aesthetically, shouldn't be next to one another.

They just look wrong to me like that, at first.

But after a while I think they look absolutely right.

That photo spread wasn't the only venue where Timothy King and John McKinney crossed paths. Across the street and a few houses down from the King residence were some of McKinney's closest friends, the Coffey family, who were consummate art collectors and had business ties to McKinney's gallery in Birmingham. John McKinney was at the Coffey house frequently, had dinners with the family, and generally mingled with them in a variety of social situations. As did Timothy King during those same years, visiting with the Coffey children.

This single degree of separation between Tim King and John McKinney, whether known by the police or not, was not discovered by the families of the victims until 2010, around the time that Cathy Broad, Tim's sister, tells me about it via email. She says that she and Pat Coffey, one of the sons, have been backtracking through their personal understanding of the OCCK case and discovered that John's younger brother had previously worked for McKinney at the art gallery as well. So McKinney can be linked to

Timothy King and also to the brother of the suspect John, who can be linked to Busch. Cathy
later tells me that another of the Coffey children,
sixteen years old at the time, used to babysit for
Jill Robinson, victim #2. McKinney was also a
patron of the Cass, placing him in proximity to
Richard Lawson.

Jill Robinson, Timothy King, John McKinney,
John, Christopher Busch, and Richard Lawson
appear to have, at most, only one degree of separation from each other, through McKinney.

WHEN I GOOGLE John McKinney's murder,
nothing immediately comes up. But I find
another John McKinney, and he's the cofounder
and president of something called the Fox Island
Lighthouse Association. I look at his picture.
This other John McKinney looks to be in his
mid-fifties, wears a parka, and has curly hair that
sweeps in the wind.

I blow the picture up and print it. I tack it to
my wall next to that of the art gallery owner. This
new photo is John McKinney's son.

FIGHTERS

I park a few blocks from the river when I get off the Lodge again, which I seem to be driving on pretty frequently, just to get down into the heart of the city and wander. I eventually make my way on foot over to the Cass. The walking clears my head but also makes me feel close to the streets, where the murders seem to rise from the concrete like heat waves sometimes, the story surrounding me as I pass through it, only now there's a slight drizzle and I pull my sweatshirt against the wetness and walk across a vacant parking lot. The attendant, a black guy in his twenties, is smoking a cigarette in his booth, and I'm the closest he's come to action all day. He must work on commission, because nobody in this city would pay him to watch these empty two hundred spaces.

I frog through traffic to the Joe Louis fist sculpture; I'm jaywalking, and a traffic cop whistles at me but I don't look. There's really no authority in a traffic cop's presence down here. They know this, blowing their whistles out of boredom only, it seems. The police down here are for life-and-death emergencies, if that. If you stop at a red light in the evening hours, you're an idiot. You slow down, you roll through the light when the traffic is clear. You will not get a ticket, since the cops expect nothing less of you. They would prefer that you roll through reds rather than getting yourself jacked at a dead stop. All that paperwork for them to take care of. All your fucking brains on the ground.

The Joe Louis fist sits in a median on Jefferson Avenue, so it's seen from automobiles driving both east and west through downtown. In the summertime, pedestrians jam the crosswalk taking pictures of it. Right now, I'm alone and I stand there looking up at the sculpture for a while. It's so big.

The sculpture of world champion boxer Joe Louis's fist and forearm is twenty-four feet long, weighs eight thousand pounds, and is cast in bronze. It hangs twenty-four feet above the ground, suspended sidelong from cables like it's punching outward, but at what?

The artists named the sculpture *Fist of a Champion*, and for decent reason. Joe Louis and his family had come to Detroit from the South in the 1920s, escaping the Ku Klux Klan. He'd lived in the Detroit ghetto area called Black Bottom. He used to hide his boxing gloves in a violin case so his mom wouldn't suspect him of trouble. Later, in 1937, Joe Louis defeated the

Cinderella Man, James Braddock, to become world champion.

What would Joe Louis think of Detroit now, in 2010, I wonder, all this time later and still in an era that finds blacks and whites segregated? An era in which I, supposedly a "man of letters," still see Black Man in Booth, White Man in Car, Hispanic Man on Corner . . . ? Maybe I am just describing people, the way I grew up doing, but have my descriptions been whitewashed? Who paid for this fist to be erected, and with whose million dollars? And why put the fist of a big black boxer in the center of a city that seems to have abandoned that boxer's very people, if it were not conceptualized from a vantage of privilege, from those outside the circle of poverty, throwing a few crumbs of culture to the people at the center?

I imagine the Joe Louis fist turning clockwise, its middle finger pointing up, turning inward at the city that built it, and that may have betrayed its promise and glory as well.

COMPACT CARS

I'm in my hotel room and it's late. I've just come from meeting with Ellie at a diner, where we sat and had ice cream and coffee. We didn't talk about my wife, and Ellie didn't ask me about the bandage on my hand, either, just placed her small hand over my own while we talked quietly.

This is something I remembered about Ellie, always: the way hurtful things—the laceration on my hand from where I'd smashed the telephone in my hotel room against it, just to feel that pain again for a second, or the breaking apart of my heart from failing at marriage, at perfection for my kids—seemed to drift away when she touched me, and Ellie knew this. When my pain wasn't caused by Ellie, Ellie soothed it.

I can't sleep after the coffee, and I mute my television and spend the next hour sitting on my hotel bed, sorting through my documents until I, by happenstance, find a hastily photocopied column from a local newspaper, circa 1977.

In it there's a description of an abduction attempt, in which a young boy was in the candy aisle of a pharmacy. He looked down the aisle and saw a middle-aged man in a rust-colored blazer staring at him. The man wore a shirt and tie under his blazer. The man's eye contact was creepy. When the boy left the store, the man was in the parking lot, where he attempted to get the boy into his car.

I lean back against my headboard and can feel the little synapses firing off under my skin. I know why people claw themselves when they're detoxing. It's been maybe a year since I've had a drink but it feels like fucking forever, a lifetime ago, since I nearly wrapped my car around a tree almost every weekend for six months straight, had largely immoral encounters outside of my marriage, said horrible things to people I actually liked. I read over the article again. It describes the man who tried to abduct me when I was a boy, the same candy aisle scenario, the same blazer, the same look on his face. He's driving the same type of car that followed me away from the shopping center, the compact that rolled up beside me a few blocks away.

That's the man that I've been thinking about all these years, but there's no way to know if he's related to the killings. There's no way to even track him. The cops didn't even have computers then. The police were still keeping notes on cocktail napkins.

I know that this part of the story is important, as much as any, but from whose eyes do I tell

100

it, the seven-year-old boy walking home from the pharmacy he'd nearly shoplifted candy at, his pockets holding on to the idea of the stolen candies that are merely symptomatic of the darker urges inside him?

It's a nicer story than some: that of an eight-year-old girl whose cage allows only glimpses of her parents as they push the saltines, her daily meal, to her, or that of a boy hustled from hand to hand at an airport in London, or the story told from inside the trunk of a car, the wheel wells ticking off the first three hours of uncertainty.

Why is my story thirty-five years ago any different than that of any other kid ten feet from a car with a man in a blazer and the presumption of power inside it?

From what vantage do I tell the clearest truth: that when a man swings open the passenger-side door and reaches out to you, it is more like an extension of the hand you already feel at home, clutching at the back of your hairline? How when you run full tilt afterward it is more like a stone leaping across water, that lightness in your head, that dark-tendriled play of hiding and seeking but with an urgency you don't have language for yet?

Is this how the story is told after decades?

I spend hours digging through old newspaper articles at the public library the next night in Southfield until they kick me out and I drive around my old neighborhood with my headlamps lighting lawns I used to walk across. I drive back to my hotel and collapse on the bed to a *Cold Case* episode about Richard Lawson and the taxicab murder he'd gone to prison for. Cory Williams, the Detroit-area cop who'd traveled to Atlanta to conduct the John interview, is himself interviewed in the episode. He seems smart and he seems to like the attention. I can hear the ice machine down the hall from me while I'm sleeping, and at three a.m. I sit up startled and can't fall back asleep until two hours later.

These experiences don't feel real somehow, as if I've made up a journey in order to follow it, purposefully away from my home and the relationship with my wife, toward something closer to what I'd felt as a boy, maybe. And in the blue of the television lighting across my bed, my heart pounding with sadness, there's the wish to be held by my father one time, to hold my own son, to beg of my daughter forgiveness for being a man in a world that would strip her of power, as Kristine had been stripped, and redress her to make nice, just because it can.

This is what wakes me up every night: It's not the ice machine, it's how seldom I feel I've loved my children right, with everything I have, and how little time is left for me to do so.

GILL ROAD

I'm eating a Coney dog with my dad in Southfield, the first time I've seen him since my uncle, his younger brother, died a few years back. My dad still has the dark features, high cheekbones, and piercing blue eyes of his youth. He's hard not to notice in a room.

Even though my dad and I don't have a good relationship, we don't let this get in the way of meeting. I'm in town and have pledged to see him. After a few years of radio silence, I feel refreshed by the idea.

I USED TO go to the American Coney in high school and to the Lafayette Coney at maybe midnight or one o'clock on a Saturday, order two or three dogs smothered in chili, onions, and mustard. The lines to order would be deep and you screamed out what you wanted over other teenagers' heads. You didn't park more than a block away or you got jumped.

There's a great picture of me in a red and white varsity jacket sitting alone at the counter in American, at midday, sometime around 1987.

My hair is in a front poof, I'm clean-shaven, and there's pudge in my cheeks. I was having sex all the time with my girlfriend back then. I wore a gold pinky ring with my initials on it, and my career goal at the time was to own shopping malls. I used to look at that picture years later, in my twenties, and think, *Who the fuck is that?*

When I look at that picture now sometimes, nearing forty, I feel hollow inside.

While the older waitress writes him out a bill, my dad bullshits with her to a point where she doesn't even understand him anymore, then she gets rude in return.

"What's her fucking problem?" he says to me when she walks away. He smiles, grinds on a toothpick with his molars.

He's wearing a sidearm, a .38 revolver, under his Michigan State University sweatshirt; Michigan State is my alma mater, so he must be wearing the sweatshirt on my account. When I tell my dad how I went to an AA meeting with my sister in the past week—one of the things we sometimes do to stay healthy, like therapy, only free—he says, "She cry over her fucking beer the whole time?"—which is odd to me, not only because I don't understand his approach to relationship building but because I've never seen my sister have a beer before; everyone in our family drinks vodka when we drink.

After lunch, we're in my dad's Monte Carlo

with a racing stripe up the middle and leather seats that smell brand-new even after five years. I've recruited him to drive me out to Gill Road in Livonia, where Timothy King's body had been found. He drives fast, showing off the Monte Carlo's horsepower while I tap at the GPS on my iPhone.

Ellie's address is in the phone, too, and I feel like talking about her but I don't. That's going to be the hard part about seeing Ellie while I'm here: feeling like I can't tell anybody about our reconnecting. Even though Ellie and I haven't slept together, I am obviously betraying my marriage, and I am worried about what that says about me. Also, I am worried about ruining what Ellie and I have started, because right now it feels good, and good is something I need in my life.

Gill Road was mostly wooded and spotty with small-acre farmland in 1977, the year Timothy King was found here. I have a worn photocopy of an old newspaper article about the discovery of Tim's body. There's a man in the photo pointing to the ditch where Tim was found. The man, maybe sixty, is standing near a grove of hardwoods thinned by winter. There's snow, and a house in the background.

Gill Road has been developed since then. Green signs mark the side streets. What used to be a dirt road is groomed pavement now. It's the grove of hardwoods, somehow preserved, that my dad recognizes before I do.

He parks, and we get out.

"Right fucking there," he says, pointing with his index finger almost like the man in the photo points, only my dad is hustling. He's excited. This is my dad making up for lost time, connecting with me, and I don't begrudge him it. This is what I wished he had done for years: come along for the ride.

I hold my Flip cam out and walk along the shoulder of the road. I hold the photo from the newspaper in front of my lens: the grove of trees, the house in the background, the indentation where a ditch had been top-dressed with snow.

When I pan to my right, it's all there, only the trees haven't thinned yet and the snow is still a couple of months away.

But I'm standing in the exact spot where Tim's body had been dumped, and it's an interesting feeling being with my dad right now to witness this. In some ways I feel like I died alongside Tim in '77, the last year my dad was beating the shit out of anybody in our home, only I'm somehow still standing. I don't know if my dad feels any of this, but he's quiet for most of the ride back to my hotel, where we sit in the car for a few minutes.

It's started to rain outside, and he runs his wipers in one clean streak before clicking them off. Then he tells me he's proud of me, but I don't know what for and I don't ask.

"I'm almost forty," I tell him.

"I know that," he says.

I take a shower later in my hotel room and then I get into my bed and don't leave it for the rest of the day. I watch cable, and at some point I'm just staring at the plasma screen with my eyes watering and the sound of rain outside.

FOX ISLAND

Lake Michigan is enormous. It moves like the sea when its waves hit the shore. Bordering the entire western side of Michigan, it's hundreds of miles long and a hundred miles wide. You can't see across it except on very clear nights and for about a week during the summer, when you can faintly recognize the Chicago skyline a five-hour drive away.

But Chicago's in the south, across a huge divide. Far to the north along Lake Michigan, off the Leelanau Peninsula, the Fox Islands are wooded and desolate, adrift in this would-be ocean. You can get to the islands only by boat or plane. In the winter, when the snow falls heavy month after month, boats will not traverse to it.

During the 1970s, a late-middle-aged man named Frank Shelden, narrow-faced and smarmy with intellect, owned the 835-acre North Fox Island privately. During summers Shelden ran a boys' camp on the island, marketed as a safe haven for reconnecting troubled and at-risk youth with the splendor of nature.

But the island had become more of a snake

pit those summers than a peak-season getaway. Children would arrive anticipating an iconic experience meant to instill a love of the wilderness, increase one's self-reliance, connect one to a higher power, and socially enlighten one to the joys of team building. Instead of that, they were routinely molested on camera, both in still and moving pictures, by Frank Shelden and other adult men on sex jaunts, either in from the suburbs of Detroit or on fuck-and-duck missions on the proverbial Cessna from other areas around the country.

There was no way for the children to escape the island. When he insisted, they slept in Frank Shelden's bed. For a while, nobody knew about it.

Like other molestation camps around the country operating similar, highly successful pornography rings that have since been well chronicled in dozens of news articles, North Fox Island even received government subsidies. Organized as a charity under the name Brother Paul's Children's Mission and billed as a child care facility, Frank Shelden's organization was eligible for $150 per month per boy from its county coffers; $400 per month per boy from the state; and $700 per month per boy from the federal government.

Brother Paul's of Fox Island, then, could rake in $1,250 per month per boy to commit among the most heinous of crimes, and all of this money was exempt from income tax by the IRS.

This was just fluff money. Pornography linked to the molestations generated even bigger business.

FRANK SHELDEN, MILLIONAIRE

A regular, secret contributor to *Better Life Monthly*, a newspaper whose own masthead dedicated it to "boy love," Frank Shelden otherwise had a clean public image and was on a variety of charitable boards, including that of the Cranbrook Institute of Science, which was associated with the very prestigious, private Cranbrook schools in the suburbs. A savvy businessman skilled in the covert ops of pedophilia, Shelden organized "sponsorship" opportunities surrounding the Fox Island retreat. In exchange for their tax-deductible contributions, nearly three hundred sponsors of the island regularly received illicit child pornography in mailers disguised to look like propaganda from the camp.

During the winter off-seasons, Frank Shelden arranged for young boys to be flown onto the island via his private plane under the promise of lavish getaways with the trusted philanthropist. There on the snow-covered island, without the company of other children, boys as young as eight years old were forced to endure the horror of Shelden's bait-and-switch techniques. They were alone. They were on an island with a middle-aged man curled around them. Insert whatever emptiness you feel, and then hold on to that for the rest of your life. You still won't even be close to feeling what those boys must have felt.

AS FAR AS locals were concerned, Frank Shelden was a prize. In addition to his work with the camp on North Fox Island, he treated favored kids to hunting trips; took them to Aspen, Colorado, for skiing ventures; held beach parties for them at a family estate in Antigua; and set up college trust funds for their educations.

Eventually, the Michigan State Police zeroed in on Fox Island after continued reference to it from multiple Detroit-area pedophiles during other, unrelated investigations. An investigation into Fox was eventually begun, quietly.

Just a few days before an arrest warrant was issued for Frank Shelden, however, he fled the country, having been tipped off. He sent one of the boys he'd molested—now eighteen years old—a postcard promising to pay for his college education. The boy, suicidal after years beneath the slithering hand of Shelden, sucked on a rifle and squeezed the trigger.

During the OCCK investigation, Fox Island

would continue to be referenced. Suspects would allude to it, and one of them would name Christopher Busch in association.

The list of Fox Island sponsors was confiscated by the Michigan State Police, rerouted through the FBI, and finally reported by the feds as accidentally destroyed in a flood—an unimaginable fate for key documents being held by one of the most organized, powerful law enforcement agencies in the world.

DRY MARTINI

Erica McAvoy, Kristine Mihelich's younger half sister, sits across from me in a booth at the Stillwater Grill at two o'clock in the afternoon. She's thirty-five years old. We're just off the interstate in Okemos, Michigan, about an hour's drive from the suburbs of Detroit.

The Stillwater is a mid-scale lunch place, like a TGI Fridays. Erica's a real estate agent. She picked this place and probably brings her clients here. She's dressed tidily, possibly to make a sale later in the day. Her haircut seems salon-styled. She orders a dry martini, and when it comes, I watch the midday sun cut across her glass from a large window to my side. I've ordered an iced tea, although I probably won't drink it. I've already had two coffees today.

A year ago I would have ordered a drink, maybe a martini like Erica's. Five years ago I would have ordered three of those martinis, sucking on olives while we talked. Fifteen years ago I would have made it a five-bourbon lunch, driven back to my hotel, and contemplated the various ways I could harm myself in a single evening. But now I have my kids to consider, and these other kids to dig up.

My iced tea comes, and Erica says, gesturing out the window, "There's my dad."

I look out the window and see her father stepping down from a large black pickup truck.

Erica hadn't told me her father was coming. She'd held back, maybe on purpose.

"I hope you don't mind me inviting him along," she says.

It's understandable that she'd want her father here. I wish I'd thought of that, getting his story alongside of hers. I'm staring at Erica's drink, knowing that I'll have to eat something but feeling the awkward impropriety of food in a situation like this. Her older sister had been held in captivity for nineteen days and eventually murdered, and I'm about to order a steak salad. I've been running on empty, but the whole performance just feels rude, looking over a menu, making small talk. Even me being here feels blasphemous.

I get out of the booth when Tom Ascroft comes in. I shake his hand. He stands about five foot seven, weighs about 160, and has a hardscrabble grip like my father used to have. In his sixties now, Tom is balding, and there's a scar ringing his crown from a surgery that I don't ask him about. I contemplate that scar over the very occasional lulls in our four-hour conversation.

Tom was Kristine's stepfather at the time of the killings. She had a biological dad somewhere around Detroit, but my understanding is that he'd been more or less absent. Tom raised Kristine and had Erica and another daughter with Kristine's mom after he joined the family.

When Tom orders an old-fashioned, he does so without even a blink, like he'd been tasting the bite of its whiskey, and the cherry-sweet chaser, before he even got here. I can smell the sweetness of his drink when it comes and I want one, too, the little rapid-fire spasms in blood chemistry egging me on.

Tom and Erica drink fast. They each order another cocktail while they talk to me about Christopher Busch. They tell me about the detectives supposedly losing evidence; they make little rabbit ears with their fingers when they say "losing." And they talk about North Fox Island and other possibly related porn syndicates.

We become quiet at the mention of Fox Island, the darkness of that place we'd each studied to the point of overkill, the influx of boys being dropped off by single-engine plane during wintertime or ferried through the crush of spring ice once the weather had warmed: None of us mentions the imagery of young skin, the flashing of camera bulbs, the ticking of 8mm film.

Later, Tom and Erica talk about being stone-walled by the Michigan State Police, the attorney general, and the various detectives and prosecutors over the years. Tom says he's felt shoved out from the beginning. He tells me about wanting to identify Kristine's body back in '77 but not being allowed to. He says he immediately went down to the morgue but was initially stone-walled because he wasn't blood related.

He was on fire, he tells me.

"I showed up," he says. He shakes his head in sadness and can't seem to say anything more.

Then, after a while, he says, "There was a detective down there, and I grabbed his gun. I took it out of his fucking holster." He tells me he waved it around and that he would have shot somebody. I nod my head, believing him. I might have shot somebody, too.

The cops let him see Kristine after they real-ized his sincerity with the weapon. One of the officers had stayed in Tom's home while the PD searched for Kristine during those nineteen days of captivity—a common precaution in case the killer rang them or showed up in person—and had intimately understood, and possibly shared, Tom's despair. There was no tussle, no arrest. Tom gave the detective his gun back and stepped into a room to view his stepdaughter. It was the 1970s, and you could do shit like that and still get away with it, still cross your fingers for personal involvement. Nowadays, Tom would be serving a decade for pulling a cop's piece.

Tom identified Kristine, still frozen in a seated position as if she were driving a go-cart on the autopsy table, but she was clothed. Whoever killed Kristine saw more of her than Tom did.

Halfway through our lunch, Tom says to me, a slight buzz in his eyes from the alcohol but also from anger, "Who knows what her clothes were covering up."

Neither of us says anything for a long few minutes. My digital recorder blinks atop the table. Erica's martini glass is dry, I notice. Her forefinger rests inside of it like a shovel inside a shed.

When we walk out of the restaurant after lunch, Tom and Erica are both a bit sauced. We shake hands in the parking lot. On the way to my rental, I glance back and see Tom stepping firmly into his truck, a bulge from the ankle of his jeans revealing the imprint of a pistol, I think.

MAGIC MAN

In the summer of 1976, in the midst of the OCCK murders, Gerald Richards, a thirty-something gym teacher at St. Joseph Catholic Elementary School in Dexter, in the suburbs, decided to run for county commissioner and enlisted the help of an eight-year-old student to pass out election pamphlets for him.

In exchange for the work, Richards promised the boy's parents that he would take the boy on a trip. Some days later, Richards picked up the boy in his car and then also picked up three other boys, all students at St. Joseph's, and headed out of town. All four boys were driven to a small airport in St. Clair County, about an hour east of Detroit, where Frank Shelden was waiting in his Cessna.

The boys were flown to North Fox Island. They landed, got into a jeep, and drove to one of Frank Shelden's cottages.

During their three-day stay, the boys took hikes, goofed around near the water, and were subjected to the usual molestations by both Shelden and Richards that occurred in Shelden's evening lair.

• • •

GERALD RICHARDS, IN addition to working in the gym at St. Joseph Catholic Elementary School, owned a massage parlor in the Detroit area, performed magic shows for local charities and birthday parties, and drove an orange Pinto with the words "Jerry the Magician" printed on the side.

As clichéd pedophiles go, he fit the bill, but there were many other awkward indicators along the way and so many blatant abuses that went unreported for a long time: Richards allegedly stared at boys in the school showers, patted their naked butts "in a guy way" (as he stated in later testimony) as they walked by, sometimes massaged their groins to "prevent injury," and occasionally "measured" boys for athletic supporters by holding on to their penises and placing a ruler beside them.

On several occasions Richards invited boys to his home on the weekends; there, a leather massage table awaited them in his basement, the windows of which had been blacked out with paint so that nobody outside could peek in.

At some point during the summer of '76, Gerald Richards took a boy to Port Huron, just minutes from the small airport where Frank Shelden normally kept his plane. An acquaintance had rented a small room at the Holiday Inn, where the boy was taken into a hotel room with both men and molested over multiple days.

Months before this, in January of 1976, only weeks before the first OCCK abduction, Richards took two other boys to Frank Shelden's home in Ann Arbor, where they, too, were routinely abused throughout the night, their stories collected and preserved in police documentation, in gruesome detail.

WHILE BOTH SHELDEN and Richards were listed as directors on official brochures for the Fox Island camp, a fifteen-year-old boy, Michael F., was highlighted alongside them as a camp counselor. Being fifteen, the boy would invoke trust in the parents of other children being considered for placement. Like Vincent Gunnels, the teenaged victim and, later, possible accomplice of Christopher Busch, Michael F. appears to have been used as a snare. Shelden and Richards, engaging in a common ruse among pedophiles, dangled the looks and youth of Michael F. in order to lure those children who might otherwise not approach.

Michael F. gave testimony about having been "friends" with Richards for approximately three years, beginning with a molestation in Richards's blacked-out basement at the age of twelve and then continuing while Michael F. worked for Richards as an assistant to his magic shows.

Over the three years of ongoing abuse, Michael F. and Richards had about a dozen sexual encounters with each other, often with a third, also under-aged party brought in to participate. Richards would make the two children take photographs and moving pictures of one another, most of this happening on North Fox Island and in Port Huron.

All photographs and film of their hundreds of victims were routincly shared between Richards and Shelden, but also among a private client list even more secreted than the island's sponsor list. This was pre-Internet, of course, and instead of monthly credit card fees for a porn site, private "philanthropic donations" were received via U.S. mail, then packages containing sample footage would be bundled by hand and shipped out discreetly.

RICHARDS IDOLIZED FRANK Shelden for his wealth and access. They first met when Richards advertised his magic show in *Better Life Monthly*, the pedophilia rag, Shelden contacting him afterward by letter. They corresponded using innuendos that revealed their shared tendencies. Shelden later financed Richards on a trip to an out-of-state convention of magicians, impressing Richards with the fluidity of his expendable income.

They eventually organized the camp together. Richards had gone from a blue-collar gym teacher driving a Pinto to hobnobbing with the elite: a private plane, a private island, and endless private parties behind dungeon doors.

By the time Richards was in police custody, he was on the verge of a nervous breakdown caused by both the disintegration of his enterprise and the certainty of prison time. Frank Shelden, following in the tradition of all great elitists, had taken his money and his private plane, abandoned the sycophant Richards, and absconded to foreign lands. Shelden at first resided at the family-owned mansion on Antigua but eventually settled in the Netherlands, a pornography hotbed, where he lived for two more decades on his family's extensive wealth.

Prior to Shelden's death in the mid-nineties, years of attempted extraditions failed. For whatever reason, the Michigan State Police, the FBI, and multiple political figures were unable to extract Frank Shelden from his power and influence, and consequently were unable to extract any justice for the hundreds of boys he molested in the United States.

GET RID OF IT

Gerald Richards gave testimony to the surface of his and Shelden's crimes together in exchange for leniency from the courts. Some of this testimony revolves around an occasion in March of 1976 when Frank Shelden, flying an underaged boy to Fox Island, put the plane on autopilot and molested the young man over the Saginaw Bay. Around this same time Mark Stebbins had been missing. While the Stebbins captivity dates reportedly preceded this incident, what's worth noting is both Shelden's activity at the time and the very real possibility of the March date being an intentional misdirect by Richards.

In addition to testimony related to their production of the still- and motion-picture pornography capturing their routine raping of victims, Richards also gave testimony to the incorporation of Fox Island by the state, the details of its charter, and its connection to two previously unheard-of shell organizations known as the Church of the New Revelation and the Oceanographic Living Institute.

The shell trusts were organized in cahoots with

two mystery characters, Dyer Grossman of both New Jersey and New York, and Adam Starchild, of reportedly unknown origin. Both names would attract media attention.

When hunted down, Dyer Grossman, wearing rectangular and thick, black-framed glasses and with a mouth like an open strawberry, would be found to have been first living in Walnut Creek, California, collecting funds as a foster parent for a boy he'd been molesting, and then later living in the Netherlands alongside Shelden. Starchild had, reportedly, remained a ghost; he had eluded police and the name couldn't be tracked.

A plethora of correspondence was provided, outlining the Fox Island financial schema that allowed it to operate tax-free with its per-child government subsidies. Other franchise-style camps were discovered to be in the planning stages by Shelden and Richards, with locations on both coasts.

Richards testified to modeling their organization on the success of like-minded operations such as Boys Farm, Inc., located in Winchester, Tennessee, and run by Reverend Claudius "Bud" Vermilye, whose credentialed (read rich) clients could be personally furnished with a young boy for an extended "vacation-type" visit.

A search warrant was eventually issued for Frank Shelden's home in an upscale Ann Arbor neighborhood, fitting for the heir to the developer of Detroit's famously extravagant Grosse Point mansions. Officers arrived, found the home vacated, and broke out a lower window to gain entry.

Richards had given officers a detailed floor plan of the home, advising that copies of film footage and photographs could be found in a series of file cabincts in an office on the lower level. In a darkened room, three file cabinets were indeed found. Reportedly, one cabinet had only papers in it, and the other two had been emptied.

Multiple known or newly discovered pedophiles residing in Michigan were questioned in relationship to the Fox Island scandal, including an elementary school principal, a child social services employee, and several directors and board members of other child welfare organizations. Eventually the investigation grazed a local police officer, a man referred to in confidential documents only as "Lindsay," who was in possession of multiple reels of child pornography as well as print photographs depicting several Fox Island boys.

Lindsay claimed not to know Frank Shelden or Gerald Richards, but, along with the pornography found in his home, there was print material from the camps and receipts from donations he'd made to the Boys Farm in Tennessee. The pornography was confiscated and eventually destroyed instead of held as evidence.

GERALD RICHARDS HAD a short stay in a psychiatric hospital while awaiting trial. During that stay, he provided statements revealing his secret ownership in a two-room naturology clinic in Port Huron, where he had previously taken two boys to meet with Frank Shelden, each on different occasions.

The location seemed inconsequential until years later when a young girl would testify to the FBI about having observed her father and other members of a pornography syndicate, one of them "someone powerful from Ann Arbor," raping and, on a few occasions, killing young children in what she called "a doctor's office."

She also testified to police officer involvement in the activities.

A case report dated June 10, 1976, many months before the final two OCCK victims would be killed, outlines information received from the Tennessee Bureau of Criminal Identification detailing a link between Boys Farm and four major sponsors noted as living in the Detroit area. Their names, ages, and places of residence have been whited out from all official documents.

Richards eventually pled as accused on multiple criminal sexual conduct charges. Several of the victimized boys, a small percentage of them, testified. Richards was sentenced to two to twenty years in prison, served ten, and by the late 1980s was a free citizen living with his mother in Michigan.

AGAINST THE WIND

Ellie and I have dinner at another diner and then go for a drive, old-school Detroit classic rock on the radio. We say nothing while I turn corners and take curves on Hines Drive along a river banked by trees. She's recently dyed her black hair even blacker and looks like Joan Jett.

We're both thinking of the same thing, I think, how years ago we used to take her baby for a cruise down Hines Drive in her Oldsmobile when we were bored that first summer we met. We'd swerve along the Rouge River and we'd have the windows down and Ellie's hair would flip in the wind all the time. We'd listen to Nirvana on the cassette player and then we'd get out and walk along the river. Ellie would hold her baby on her hip and toss chunks of balled-up Wonder Bread to the ducks. When Ellie wanted to smoke, I'd hold her baby and try to remember being held like that but couldn't. It hurt to think I could give my love to a baby that wasn't mine while being cheated out of that same love from a father who'd had the opportunity but didn't take it.

I never wanted to let Ellie's baby go. I used to

129

smell her hair all the time, pressed beneath my chin while I carried her, and it made me weak.

In the wintertime, Ellie and I started listening to Courtney Love's band, Hole.

A lot later, after we'd split, I used to drive down Hines by myself and feel the hurt all over again, pushing that cassette into my player.

It's been so many years, and all of this time I've been holding on to Ellie like I might have held on to the memory of my father or of Hines Drive or anywhere else that promised me sanctuary.

When I drive back to her place to drop her off, we sit in my SUV and I turn the radio down and we talk.

The light from the radio tints her hand electric blue when it crosses to my knee. We still haven't slept together, and I want to, but also I won't. I don't know what Ellie wants. I can feel us moving in a current together, and that frightens me, but I say nothing and neither does she.

We just sit like that outside her home for a while, and then when I'm on the freeway going back to my hotel, I decide to take a different exit and drive the twenty minutes to Troy.

I measure out the distance along I-75 with my odometer and then pull onto the shoulder in the dark where, based on newspaper clippings, I can assume Jill Robinson, the second victim, had been dumped.

I put my blinkers on and get out.

There's a huge wind that rattles my SUV when a semitruck passes, and then the air is still and silent and no cars pass for a while. In the distance I can see the lights of commercial businesses, the Troy PD, and the massive Somerset Collection mall complex; but when I turn my back to the city, everything ahead is dark.

I stand in a ditch beyond the shoulder. A few cars pass. Somebody slows and then speeds up again. I can see the ditch willows in his taillights, and it feels like summer suddenly, how when you were a teenager you used to find yourself outside in the middle of the night the way adults don't do.

Or the way, when I was a little older, I used to make out with Ellie on the hood of my car, how I'd press my body against her jeans and hear her breathing become shallow, then quicken suddenly, and how everything was so humid all the time when we were together.

Like in that Bob Seger song, "Against the Wind," nothing mattered to us but each other. That time in our lives lasted only a blink, but we were young and strong, or at least wanted to be, and the whole fucking thing was before us, waiting for us to inhabit it, whatever that thing was.

But then the moment ended, like everything else. We dated maybe eighteen months, but it felt like five minutes and it felt like my entire life at the same time.

Ellie had been what I'd planned for, right before she was gone.

I can't know specifically what Jill Robinson had planned for in her own life, but standing there in the high grass and the north-leaning willows on the side of the road with nothing but darkness and taillights and the damp smell of ditch weeds and gasoline in the air, I know that Jill Robinson would have been planning for a lot, for the million little moments that make up a world, and that we never expect to be taken from us before they are.

HIT MEN

C hristopher Busch, the suspect who reportedly shot himself without leaving gunshot residue, was the son of a prominent Detroit family. A food service worker in his mid-twenties, he primarily lived off his parents, enjoying their automobiles, their homes, and the small restaurant his father invested in so that Christopher could have a job.

At five feet eight inches and 250 pounds, Christopher was fantastically barrel-shaped and his beard went down to his neckline. The hair on his head was greasy. His skin was pale.

His father, H. Lee Busch, was the chief financial officer for General Motors' entire North Atlantic division. Before the car company bailouts of our recent recession, many of us were beginning to think of General Motors as a doomed enterprise, overwhelmed by inefficiencies and improbable debt, but in its heyday of the 1970s, General Motors had a greater revenue stream than most small countries.

Even the lowliest of GM employees, of the hundreds of thousands of them in the auto industry at large, would clock $40,000 in a calendar year working regular hours on the assembly line. That was great money in the 1970s. There were guys everywhere with only a GED putting in overtime and buying up second homes, mostly wilderness cabins an hour or two north of the blue-collar concrete grids that kept them employed.

As an executive in that world, H. Lee Busch had more than just money. He had access and power, and it trickled down to his kids.

We didn't have any of that when I was growing up. We lived in the low-mortgage Oak Park area at first during my early childhood. A couple years later, somebody on our block bought a used, beat-to-hell limousine for their daily driver and parked it on the lawn. My father saw that as a sign that the neighborhood was "turning ghetto," and we eventually moved to another small house a few miles away, in Southfield, when I was five.

My brother, in turn, was smoking weed, listening to acid rock on the eight-track player in the basement-level bedroom he'd eventually moved his quarters to, escaping the original bunk bed he'd first shared with me, and nursing the wounds my father would inflict. I think my brother probably sees it differently all these years later, time having softened some of the blows, the soldier in him having thickened his body and hardened his jaw and mind to the blows that could not be softened.

I don't remember spending much quality time

with my dad during those years, but on Thursday nights he occasionally sat on the bottom bunk with me and we watched the boxing competitions on a small television atop my bureau. I remember wanting to hold on to those moments with him. My dad knew a lot about boxing. He'd grown up in Detroit proper, was a "greaser" who had gravitated vicariously to the roughness of the streets. He was lean with muscle, his knuckled fists cutting and jabbing through the glow of my bedroom while he taught me the trade, telling me to put up my hands while he punched at them during commercial breaks.

I felt the sting of his fists against my palms, and I liked it because it seemed to be the only time my dad ever touched me.

THOMAS "THE HITMAN" Hearns was a widely popular boxer back then. He was tall like my dad and decisive with a strike. He had trained at the Kronk Gym in Detroit and eventually become a world champion. My dad was obsessed with him. There was something in the way Hearns hit that spoke to my dad with a force that family couldn't. I understand this now. It's a glorious thing to watch a boxer in his prime.

Hearns must have been what my dad seemed to feel he had missed out on: a stab at greatness, maybe. Shortly after Hearns won the national Golden Gloves light welterweight championship in '77, my dad moved out. He took my little television with him, and my mom put a fish tank on the bureau instead.

I'd lie in the bottom bunk, snapping my switchblade open and staring at the backlit fish tank. The blue and red neon of it flatlined above imitation pebbles. The Plexiglas box glowed like my old television.

Years later, I would recognize this same distance between myself and neon, alone at bars, still confused about my life, still wanting to hurt somebody just to get out of my head for a minute.

DURING WINTER BREAK when I was seven, my mom drove us through the suburbs of Birmingham and Bloomfield to look at the Christmas lights.

I guess she thought it would make us feel better, seeing the big homes lit up. Our own little brick house was the size of some of those garages and half as tall.

Christopher Busch had grown up in one of those "spreads," as my mother called them.

While I was staring through the window of our station wagon, my breath fogging across the glassy December tinsel that streamed by, my forefinger etching downward through the moisture as though marking out time, a suitcase full of 8mm film showcasing children was somewhere in Christopher Busch's possession. And just under a year later, Christopher Busch and two accomplices would plead guilty to multiple counts of criminal sexual conduct related to dozens of child molestations in areas north of Detroit.

The accomplices, less moneyed than Christopher Busch, received multiple years in prison for the crimes. One of them got life, but Christopher Busch, under the tutelage of his politically entrenched father and an expensive attorney, received only probation and a $1,000 fine.

Kristine Mihelich and Timothy King, victims #3 and #4, had not yet been killed.

Christopher Busch, out on probation at the time of their murders, was questioned several times about the OCCK murders. The suitcase full of pornography previously confiscated as evidence in the sexual misconduct charges he had faced had somehow disappeared from police custody and was no longer evidence to anything but the fact that more than just children in the OCCK case could turn up missing.

Within weeks of being polygraphed about the case, Christopher Busch was dead of the reported suicide. His father, H. Lee, incinerated Christopher Busch's body. He would do the same to the family's birth certificates shortly after-ward, for unspecified reasons.

LIAR LIAR

During the initial weeks of the OCCK investigation, two different tips were called in on Christopher Busch. Of the roughly 20,000 original tips, the Christopher Busch tips were numbers 369 and 1,035. They had come early.

Tip #369 reportedly went missing—although I would later find it—but tip #1,035 had a note attached to it stating that Busch was currently under indictment for the sexual misconduct charges mentioned, stemming from incidents with young boys at various locations. Among them was the family-owned cabin on Ess Lake, a few hours north of Detroit.

Of the hundreds of official polygraphs given during the OCCK case, Christopher Busch's was the only one attended by a prosecutor and the only time in memory that the Oakland County deputy prosecutor himself had ever made an appearance at a polygraph. Something about this particular examination demanded the presence of a higher authority.

Busch would also be polygraphed by Lawrence "Larry" Wasser, but the examination would be paid for and administered privately by his own attorneys, who, according to the King family, buried the results. Busch's official polygraph was now administered by Ralph Cabot and concerned only the murder of victim #1, Mark Stebbins. He was not questioned about victim #2, Jill Robinson. Due to her taking a shotgun wound postmortem, police allegedly weren't immediately convinced that Jill's murder was a related killing.

What was passed down the chain of command from polygraphist to the police to the press, and eventually to the families of the victims, was that Christopher Busch had passed the Stebbins polygraph. In reality, he had failed it, although nobody on the outside would know this until three decades later.

Busch couldn't be touched. He was released from questioning until future court dates on pending charges against him related to the Ess Lake molestations. His evasion of custody early on is noteworthy, as, later, police would be searching for that blue compact car, a Gremlin with a white hockey stripe—the car from the fliers plastered everywhere. The Gremlin would be seen at the abduction site of Timothy King, the OCCK's final known victim. Christopher Busch, out on his own recognizance after the Stebbins polygraph, was driving around in a 1977 two-door blue Chevy Vega, a near duplicate to the

AMC Gremlin, with white stripes down its sides.

He'd purchased the car just weeks prior to the first OCCK abduction.

THIRTY YEARS LATER, one of Christopher Busch's molestation victims was living in a half-way house in Detroit. In 2008 he gave statements to police about Busch and Gregory Greene, one of Busch's associates in the sexual misconduct charges. Greene's name had been OCCK tip #370, alongside Busch's. Tip #370 had been "lost," too, just like the first tip on Busch.

Greene, in his twenties in 1976–77, was clean-shaven and had a strong jawline and piercing eyes that were sometimes augmented by thick black-framed glasses. Greene's hair was slick and dark. He was often transient in the years prior, flitting back and forth from Michigan to California, before colluding with Busch.

The molestation victim divulged in his 2008 statements that Busch and Greene often used him as bait, like Shelden and Richards used Michael F., to lure other children to Busch's vehicle. He stated that Christopher Busch, in the winter of 1977, had once driven him and another young boy down to Detroit from the Ess Lake cottage and made the two of them perform sex acts with each other in a wooded area while Busch watched.

Busch then drove them both toward Pontiac,

forty minutes from Detroit, where he dropped off the boy from the cottage at the house of another man, the pedophile named Ted Lamborgine, who, by the time of the victim's statements to police in 2008, was serving prison time for reportedly unrelated molestation charges.

The victim stated that he believed, back in 1977, that the boy who had been handed over to Lamborgine was Timothy King. He'd believed that since the time of the molestations themselves, when he was still a child and providing his original testimony about Busch's molestation of him. The police had shown him pictures of two boys lying on tables, dead. He had recognized one of them as the King boy but kept this to himself over the years out of fear.

He also said that Busch kept handcuffs and a pistol in his blue Vega. At some point Busch himself had shown him a Polaroid of the boy who he later understood was also Timothy King. The photo had shown King tied up in the Vega's trunk.

At the time of the victim's statements in 2008, he was a grown man in his forties and was not being investigated for any crimes. Both Busch and Greene, his previously convicted molesters, were long dead. No unscrupulous motivating factors could be found for his testimony. The narrative report, written by the cop who took his statement in 2008, was not released to the press, and no further case summary or documentation appears to exist that would indicate further scrutiny or investigation based on his narrative.

I scan the narrative into an email and send it to a friend of mine in D.C. so there's backup in case my life gets muddied—in case what happens to me on the outside is what happens to me on the inside almost every day, even before studying this case: the little moments when you disappear from the world, are snatched into corners.

When I flatten my hand to the nightstand in the hotel after hitting send, I am wondering which will hurt more: the pocketknife in my gym bag or the darkness of the room when I turn down for the night.

WAYNO

Mark Wayno was twelve years old in 1977, the year after victim #1, Mark Stebbins, was murdered. Wayno, like Stebbins, went missing from the Ferndale area. He disappeared on a Monday night and police went frantically from door to door in their hunt for the boy, fearing the worst.

Wayno was five feet tall, weighed a hundred pounds, and had brown hair and brown eyes. The newspaper photos showed him to resemble both Stebbins and Timothy King. When he disappeared, Mark Wayno was wearing blue corduroy slacks, a blue pullover sweater, and a blue knit hat with matching knit gloves.

His father was so certain that Mark Wayno was dead that he publicly called for vengeance on the killer.

But two days later the Wayno boy was found alive. He claimed he'd run away and had spent two nights sleeping inside a shopping mall. He was hungry but unharmed. When found, he'd been riding a bicycle along I-75. Mark Wayno returned to his father, where they lived in their house directly across the street from the Stebbins home.

People disappear all the time. Occasionally they come back in one piece, sometimes in a few. When you set out to prosecute, you start to gather facts, but survivors, especially children, are not often forthcoming.

The most common thing an abductor says to his victim is: "If you tell on me, I will kill your family." Very few children tell after hearing this. It's the oldest trick in the book, and by far the most effective.

We do not know, after all, where Mark Wayno really was during those two days he was absent from the same block as Mark Stebbins, their homes within spitting distance.

FUCK

H. Lee Busch and his wife were described by many as being cold to their four children, occasionally pawning them off on European boarding schools such as the Le Rosey institute in Switzerland. Three of their four children predeceased the parents, one from an overdose, one from rumored complications with AIDS, and Christopher Busch from the gunshot wound.

H. Lee reportedly had an intolerance for his boys that may have stemmed from his own transgressions and subsequent self-loathing. Barry King, Timothy's dad, told me that he had heard rumors that Bobby Moore, Theodore Lamborgine's roommate, had procured young boys for H. Lee. These accusations, if true, would provide a much greater understanding of how H. Lee and Mrs. Busch could morally adapt to the consequences of using their political influence to repeatedly spring their son from trouble instead of attempting to get him help.

They had posted bond for Christopher several times on a number of molestation arrests over the years and were known to have paid off children and their families related to horrifying incidents that, because of their cash flow, had been quieted.

One of the victims, who would later become a sidekick to Busch and Greene, stated that Mrs. Busch once showed up in his squat neighborhood in a darkened limousine, requesting his silence and offering an envelope full of money.

The Busch family had an understanding of how to present a proper image, do whatever was necessary to mask indignities, and move forward. The children gained an understanding that money could buy them not only their own freedom but, in Christopher Busch's case, the silence of anyone he chose to zero in on.

His exploits peaked during periods when H. Lee and Mrs. Busch were in Europe, which were frequent due to H. Lee's position with General Motors. When the folks were gone, Chris Busch had full rein of his childhood home, the cars, and the cabin in Ess Lake four hours north, a straight shot east of the Fox Islands.

BUSCH BONDED OUT of the sexual misconduct charges on March 4, 1977. Timothy King was abducted twelve days later, on March 16, and it would be six days before his body was found. Three days into King's captivity, an anonymous caller placed Christopher Busch at the cottage in Ess Lake with two young boys. This would seem

146

to align with the 2008 witness recounting his time with Busch and the boy whom he'd thought to be King, how they had first been at the cottage together.

The caller, a middle-aged woman, spoke with a local Montmorency County sheriff's department employee on March 19.

The caller was specific about wanting to speak with a Detective Junior Brandenburg, who had originally arrested Busch on the sexual misconduct charges and had previously searched the cottage to find two shotguns, three-quarters of a pound of marijuana, and the two now-missing suitcases that had contained both the child pornography and rope-style ligatures.

The sheriff's department employee indicated that Brandenburg was out and that a message could be taken. The caller replied, "No. By then it will be too late." The caller was then heard speaking with someone in the background, who advised her against divulging more information. The caller, without giving greater detail, begged the employee to send somebody out to the Busch family cottage.

The employee stated in a report that the female caller seemed sober and serious but refused to divulge more information, so there was no rush put on the call. Timothy King's body was found three days later, on March 22. Nobody had been sent to the cottage, and the incident report of the call was not passed to Brandenburg until March 24, two days after Timothy's murder.

TWO MONTHS PRIOR to this, during the sexual misconduct interrogations in January, Gregory Greene—not having the benefit of political connections or powerful attorneys—gave up Christopher Busch as the killer of Mark Stebbins, victim #1.

That same day, in another office, Christopher Busch was being questioned by Michigan State Police detectives for the second time. Greene's betrayal had been relayed. When asked about it, Busch denied involvement in the Stebbins murder but told detectives that he and Greene had often discussed fantasies of kidnapping a boy, tying him up, and sexually abusing him.

Busch stated that, in the fantasy, either he or Greene would work their regular job at night and the other would work during the day, so that somebody would always be with the boy. When detectives asked what Busch and Greene had imagined they would do with the boy when they were done with him, Busch didn't answer.

While Busch was talking to investigators about being a pedophile, noting the usual areas he seduced boys away from, luring them into his vehicle, he named the first three OCCK abduction sites, their exact locations in the blue-collar suburbs at 9 Mile and Woodward in Ferndale,

148

13 Mile and Woodward in Royal Oak, and the 7-Eleven store on 12 Mile in Berkley. Even with this information, Busch was bonded out on the sexual misconduct charges and no further OCCK link was sought after the polygraph he'd reportedly passed.

Greene had reportedly passed one as well. Presumably his own polygraph would have included the statements he'd made about Busch and Mark Stebbins. Until 2010, news media and the public remained completely unaware of Christopher Busch's existence as a suspect, and yet he had implicated himself by claiming the exact OCCK abduction locations as his prowling grounds, had multiple pending molestation charges, had been in possession of binding ligatures and child pornography, had confessed to having fantasies of abducting children, and had been given up by his accomplice for the murder of victim #1.

If not for H. Lee's prestige in the General Motors family, it's likely that Christopher Busch would have downgraded his living quarters to the inside of a prison cell. At the very least, news media and the families of the victims would have been informed of the mounting incriminating evidence against him, with further investigation pressed on the PD.

But none of that happened. The ligatures and child pornography were either negligently lost or intentionally destroyed within custody, Christopher Busch's statements were buried, and his accomplice was put away for life, silenced behind concrete and bars.

WHITED OUT

The Busch family home in Bloomfield, thirty minutes from where I grew up, was massive and tidy at the corners. At the time of Christopher Busch's reported suicide, his parents were in England, visiting an older brother, David, with whom they'd had a falling-out over his homosexuality. Christopher Busch's penalty of probation and a $1,000 fine had recently been handed down on the sexual misconduct charges, and he'd been staying at the family residence by himself.

The Busches' regular cleaning lady arrived and tried to gain entry to the house but couldn't. She had no house key, and Christopher wasn't answering the door. She called Christopher's older brother, Charles, to let her in. In their conversation, she told Charles that something didn't feel quite right. For some reason, according to the police narratives I've been studying for months, Charles then called the police instead of simply driving over to check on the house himself.

As we know, Christopher Busch was found lying in bed next to the rifle that had presumably

151

killed him. Across the room from him, a painting on the wall had multiple bullet holes through it. A newspaper was found open to the movie section, as if Busch had been making plans for the night.

His attorney at the time, a powerhouse named Jane Burgess, would later be quoted as saying to the police upon Busch's death, in reference to the OCCK case, "You don't have to worry about it anymore." While not explicitly stating that Christopher Busch had been guilty of the OCCK murders, she'd clearly insinuated that his parting might rightly prompt an end to further investigation.

Prior to that, while defending Busch, Burgess was paid extensively and flown around the state on private planes to post Busch's bonds and meet court appointments for him. In 2007, Jane Burgess's husband—she had died by then—stated that they'd received quite a bit of money from Busch's father, who "was more concerned with the family being humiliated publicly . . . than [with] trying to help [Busch] with his problem."

The same police report that quotes Burgess's husband also indicates that three new police examiners had been brought in in 2007 to review the original Busch and Greene polygraphs, administered by Ralph Cabot in 1977, for flaws in the interpretation of the tests' results. The confidential police statement about those poly-graphs, after their 2007 audit, reads:

After a lengthy review of Busch and Greene's polygraph charts, they scored these charts and collectively came to the same conclusion, that . . .

The rest of the page is whited out, the consensus hidden from public consumption.

GETTING OUT

I learn that Vincent Gunnels, whose name I first heard in connection to the hair found on Kristine, is also the boy whom Christopher Busch's mother approached in her limousine in Flint, offering cash for his silence, presumably about her son molesting him. My file on Gunnels is splayed across the table at a Starbucks at midday, and I wonder about the possibility that Busch's mother had been attempting to silence Gunnels about more than the molestation—that, in addition to being a victim, he'd been used as a lure in the OCCK abductions, and that she'd known or suspected as much.

Given the picture that we have of the Busch family, it's easy to see the mother figure in her limousine, luxuriously detached from the horrific realities of her son's behavior. She would have seemed an iconic, impenetrable symbol of power to the young Gunnels, who was only fifteen at the time.

In 2009, Gunnels's ex-cellmate gave testimony to four months of conversations they'd had while incarcerated together. Gunnels, he said, had confided about having been "molested by a guy that killed multiple people," adding, "The victims were kids." Gunnels was out on parole during that testimony, living in Butte, Montana, at a homeless shelter. Of interest is that Gunnels's DNA was taken while he was still in prison, but the sample was backlogged at Quantico, the FBI analysis lab. Gunnels had been paroled and allowed to leave the state by the time a match had been made to the hair on Kristine.

After testimony from his ex-cellmate, representatives from local, state, and FBI offices traveled from Michigan to Montana, where they interviewed Gunnels at the Butte County Sheriff's Office. They explained to him that his DNA matched the hair they'd found. They showed him a picture of Kristine and studied his reaction. He closed his eyes and refused to look at the photograph.

He was polite, did not deny or confirm any charges that were suggested, and requested a lawyer. Officers agreed to provide him with an attorney but in the meantime assured him that they were aware of his young age at the time of the murders. They suggested to Gunnels that, by maintaining his silence about anything he might know, Busch and Greene were continuing to victimize him years after their deaths.

Gunnels made a phone call from the jail to his sister. The call was recorded and transcribed. At some point his sister repeated back to Gunnels, "Your DNA was on one of the victims." He responded by saying, "I wasn't there when it happened."

Gunnels ended up back in Michigan, imprisoned for a while on parole violations. He was freed in February of 2011 with no OCCK charges pending against him.

In 2012, information about Gunnels was finally leaked to the press. In addition to local reporters, two family members of the victims reached out to Gunnels for further questioning about the murders. He remained silent, like a lot of us fighting to get rid of a past: We simply won't talk about it.

"I'm out," we say. "I'm getting the fuck out."

And it's the only thing we can do to move forward.

FATHER FIGURE

The sexual misconduct charges that Christopher Busch and the two other men had faced stemmed from the systematic sexual exploitation of an estimated thirty boys, aged ten to fourteen, in multiple areas along the multilane, massive I-75 freeway toward the Fox Islands.

One of those areas, Flint, Michigan, became infamous in 1989 after the documentary film director Michael Moore chronicled its collapsing economy in his movie *Roger & Me*, about the auto industry abandoning that city and leaving behind ghost villages. Homes in Flint had been vacated by the block. Manufacturing facilities that had cost millions to build had been gutted for scrap; they rotted like quarter-mile-long whale carcasses beached along the city's concrete edges. The city's infamy spiked again in 2015 after the discovery that its residents had been subjected to more than a year and a half of untreated lead exposure from a fractured water system.

Gregory Greene, arrested alongside Busch, was a twenty-seven-year-old resident of Flint, already on probation for criminal sexual conduct in California a year earlier. He had been charged in Huntington Beach with sodomy of children, granted a suspended sentence, and allowed to leave the state to finish out his probation.

In Michigan, Greene reported regularly to his probation officer, maintained employment, and participated in mental health treatment. He also regularly engaged in oral and anal penetration of a preteen boy he coached on a baseball team.

In sentencing documents, Greene stated that the routine molestations of the twelve-year-old ballplayer were more for companionship than sex. "I was like a father figure to him," he stated. "He was someone I could get close to, to tell about my problems." The victim, for his part, stated that he never told anyone about Greene because Greene bragged that, in California, he had once choked, presumably to death, a boy who'd been planning on turning Greene in.

Before serving prison time on the sexual misconduct charges, Greene had worked as a night janitor at a Kmart. He was obsessive-compulsive, had an above-average intelligence, and claimed a fear of women due to experiences with his mother in childhood. Court documents assess his molestations to have been mechanical and ritualistic.

Gregory Greene's inmate identification photo and multiple mug shots betray a very solid likeness to the now-famous composite sketch that circulated Detroit during the thirteen months spanning the OCCK murders. The composite had a photo of a suspect, his description, and a likeness of that blue Gremlin he'd been seen standing beside on the night of Timothy King's abduction.

Greene's 1974 arrest in California stemmed from forty to fifty charges of child molestation, false imprisonment, and attempted murder. During his California intake interviews, Greene named fifteen young male victims whom he'd sodomized, adding that he had probably molested them over two hundred times in total. His victims ranged in age from six to fourteen.

Greene told police that he'd worked with a pedophile friend who ran a local baseball league, allowing Greene to coach in exchange for Greene bringing him young boys to molest. The California arrest came after Greene had driven a twelve-year-old boy to a wooded area skirting Los Angeles under the guise of Greene needing to momentarily retrieve a bicycle he'd left behind on a different occasion. In the woods, Greene attempted to molest the boy, who then became uncooperative. Greene got carried away. Out of frustration he struck the boy in the neck. The boy struggled further. Greene stated that he then held a hand over the boy's mouth until "he was quiet."

The boy stopped moving and Greene wasn't sure whether the boy was unconscious or dead. He pushed a lit cigarette into the boy's belly three times to see if the boy would wake up. He didn't. Greene then dragged the boy through the woods and threw him facedown into his car. He drove around Los Angeles, listening to his radio and trying to figure out what to do with the boy. Eventually, Greene dumped the boy outside of a hospital and drove away.

The boy survived, but the method of operation here fit the OCCK murders in regard to the age of the victim, method of suffocation, and the subsequent dumping of the body where it could be easily found.

Even after confessing in a manner that would implicate himself in habitual molestation, attempted murder, and a variety of other charges, Greene avoided serious prison time and was instead sent to a psychiatric hospital in Patton, California, where he stayed for less than a year. He was released into his own custody and in the summer of 1975 traveled to Michigan, where he somehow connected with Busch six months prior to the first OCCK murder.

After Busch was found dead and Greene was sentenced to a life term for the Flint molestations, the OCCK Task Force shut down. No more related murders occurred. Greene died while institutionalized.

• • •

GREGORY GREENE, ORIGINALLY from Flint, appeared to have come from a home in which his immediate needs were met. He attended a parochial school, St. Agnes High. Although his mother died during his junior year, he graduated on time. He continued to live with his father, a senior employee at one of the many Flint auto plants that eventually closed. According to Greene, his father and mother had loved him and given him a moral understanding of right and wrong. His brother, however, also had a "sex problem," Greene had said in police interviews.

During his eventual incarceration in Michigan on the sexual misconduct charges, Gregory Greene took multiple career development classes, as well as courses in radiology, management, advanced first aid, and personal and family survival, receiving certificates of achievement for each. He is quoted in his offender file as enjoying baseball, swimming, leatherwork, and reading the Bible.

He told an investigator, "For a long time I have been lost. My thinking has been screwed up. I am an intelligent person. I've accepted Christ and that has given me a whole new outlook on life."

He died of an apparent heart attack shortly thereafter.

TRIP WIRES

The Boy Scouts of America has faced thousands of victims coming forward in sexual battery cases against its organization, detailing horrific molestations inflicted upon them in the years of their youth by troop leaders and publicly calling for mass indictment of the organization's officers. Prior to these allegations surfacing, the Boy Scouts, as America's largest youth program, with over four million members, was perceived to be organized and run with the highest moral direction. Behind Boy Scout conference room doors, it appears, secreted files on known molesters within the organization's ranks, spanning almost every state in the country, were given lip service for decades: insincerely discussed by higher-ups, then set aside.

Like most of our great institutions, the Boy Scouts of America has benefited from old-money philanthropic support toward its operating expenses and acquisition of land. Its Rifle River Scout Canoe Base, located 170 miles north of Detroit along I-75, purchased its surrounding acreage from the Consumers Power Company in 1967 for pennies on the dollar. At the time, Consumers Power was the largest energy conglomerate in the United States; as such, its board members enjoyed the luxury of a monopoly and were politically entrenched in Michigan politics.

The energy elite in Detroit, along with the heads of the Big Three automakers—GM, Ford, and Chrysler—also enjoyed the endorsements of a secretive "boys' club" headquartered nondescriptly, like the Schvitz. Named the Yondotega and hidden behind unkempt concrete walls deep in the city proper, the club served as a gathering place for the international elite who dined and gamed within its sanctity. I find online that membership of the Yondotega goes back nearly a century and is limited to 150 persons total, seats being vacated only after previous members have died.

Princes and emperors, ambassadors and dukes, and captains of industry all celebrated toasts, dined on imported cuisine, and bested one another at dominoes while the city outside them slowly ravaged itself. The Rockefellers, Lindberghs, Fords, Dodges, Trumans, Hoovers, and Roosevelts all dined at the Yondotega alongside visiting aristocracy, as did a man named Russell Alger, a lumber tycoon whose wealth allowed him a seat as governor of Michigan in 1884, as well as a later appointment by President McKinley as secretary of war in 1892, and then a U.S. Senate seat in 1902.

Russell Alger's son, Frederick Alger, was appointed by President Eisenhower as ambassador to Belgium in the 1950s. Frederick Alger, enjoying the political fruits of the dynasty he had been born into, also bore the dubious distinction of becoming great-uncle to Frank Shelden of Fox Island infamy, in line for his own seat at the Yondotega when enough of its previous members had died.

The Consumers Power Company, spearheaded by W. A. Foote in 1910, had spawned its own, equally aristocratic legions. Its sons were among the most powerful in Michigan, mingling with the fraternity of the Yondotega. In the 1970s, Frank Shelden's contemporaries at the Consumers Power Company began development of a nuclear energy plant in Midland, nestled in the Flint Tri-Cities region where Christopher Busch would later be discovered to have been running boys for the elite.

SOME MEN ARE just born into money and power. Occasionally, however, a boy comes from nothing, builds himself from the ground up, crafts the universe to his will, and, against all odds, infiltrates the inner circles normally reserved by nepotism. Sometimes the money and power turn him. But other times his morality and work ethic forever betray him as an outsider, regardless of wealth.

Ed Cole, the former head of General Motors, was somebody who had come from nothing and gained the world. His access to the inner circle was suspect, likely even to himself. But even the best of us get used to things going our way, until they don't. In May of 1977, Ed Cole's small plane went down in the north of the state, near Mendon, Michigan. A skilled pilot, like Shelden, Ed Cole presumably made an error in the light fog, common to Michigan, and was killed.

Cole's photo in the Birmingham newspaper article, tacked to my wall, appears immediately to the left of Timothy King's, with John McKinney on the other side. Shortly after Cole's death, the Rifle River Scout Canoe Base was renamed the Edward N. Cole Canoe Base, in recognition of Cole's long dedication to the Boy Scouts of America.

I'm in my hotel room piecing this together, sensing there's a link between Ed Cole and, at the very least, an insidious vein within Michigan society circles. I can't sleep because of the suspicion but also because the deeper I get into the case, the more I think about my own family and what we didn't have and what we did, how we survived and how we didn't.

I call my brother from my cell phone, sitting on the hotel bed with my back to the wall and my eyes closed. He'd gone to Iraq a few years ago as a combat engineer, searching in the dead of night for desert-colored trip wires rigged to explosives. I'd kept tabs on him through his blog, updated between mission sets. There were stories of improvised bombs implanted amid the carcasses of pigs, rabid dogs shot in the head at point-blank range, mortars that rained down in the night. There were photos of my brother in wraparound shooting glasses and desert camo and with his rifle, the serial number of which he would later get tattooed on his upper arm.

Sometimes my brother slept through the bombings of their compound, people dying a few hundred yards away while he snuck in a nap, most of them just kids he'd never gotten to know the names of, although he'd passed them between errands on the operating base.

I'd emailed my brother once, after hearing that another boy had been killed.

"What did he look like?" I'd asked.

A week later my brother responded: "Like me. Only younger."

FOLLOW THE BLOOD

I'm driving around Cathy Broad's old neighborhood in Birmingham, holding my Flip
cam out the window, when I stop in front of her
and Timothy's old house. It's modest in com-
parison to the many larger homes on her block.
Cathy's father, Barry King, still lives here, in
the home where he suffered after the loss of his
son.

Barry King is suing the Michigan State Police
because he believes they've been lying to him
about who killed Timothy. Thirty-odd years of
being derailed and danced around has led him
to the idea of a cover-up. He was a successful
lawyer himself, so he knows which questions to
ask of whom, and how exactly to ask them, but
the Michigan State Police have not been forthcoming.

For decades, Barry King gave the Michigan
State Police the benefit of the doubt, but reality
eventually sank in. A lot of evidence, too much of
it to ignore, has been concealed from the families
of the victims. This doesn't prove that the MSP
knows who was responsible for the OCCK

167

murders, but it does mean that an old man might die without knowing how close investigators have come to finding out—and they're damned close right now, if not sitting on top of it with their hands over their ears.

I want to knock on King's door and talk to him. Cathy has phoned ahead, telling her father to expect me in the coming days, but I'm distracted. My sister lives nearby and I haven't seen her since I've been back. I sit in my SUV for a while, idling. Since I don't have an appointment set up with Barry yet, I turn the SUV around in the King family driveway, then travel the two miles to my sister's home.

MY SISTER AND I lost touch completely for a few years. In my thirties I would try to call, but her voice mail would be full. She'd get back to me a few weeks later, at three a.m., when my phone was turned off, and leave long messages I'd wake up to in the morning. I'd try to call her back and get her voice mail again. I always imagined her exactly as she'd been as a teenager and into her twenties: long, dark hair relaxing nonchalantly down her shoulders, the high cheek-bones never calling for accentuation, eyes like a poor man's nightmare.

I saw her at my uncle's funeral and she looked weakened, having lost weight from her normal 135 pounds. She wore large sunglasses that she hid behind. She wobbled once, that I saw, during the funeral services, fatigued by grief, although certainly not entirely grief over my uncle's passing. My sister, like myself, carried a heaviness inside that sometimes had little to do with circumstance.

When I stop by her house after videotaping the King residence, I have to wait in the street to get up my courage. I'm thinking about the only photograph I have of my sister that seems truly happy. She's seventeen, in her boyfriend's red and white varsity jacket, and she's posing with our dad at a carnival in the fall. She's wearing our dad's cowboy hat set atop her head: briefly, only for the photo. There's a huge smile on her face and a flicker of joy in her eyes. Her body seems to be arcing backward slightly—toward our father, just a step behind her; toward a wished-for affection.

TWENTY YEARS AFTER that photo was taken, just before my uncle's funeral, my sister and I are in New Orleans together for a wedding. We're having drinks at a street-side bar. My sister's eyes, polished-looking and dilated, are drifting across Bourbon Street. They remind me of my mother's eyes in those early days, just after my dad left, when we were always broke, always on the verge of running out of gas. We would go to the filling station up the road from our house, at Eleven and

Evergreen, and my mom would send me inside with a wrinkled baggie of quarters while she pumped the fuel into our car, too embarrassed to chunk down the week's worth of change herself. I'd stand at the fan belt–covered counter inside, wait with my hands in my pockets while the attendant waded through my clumsily spilled coins, the nine or ten dollars that would fill our tank. When I glanced back at the car I could see my mom's Paul Mitchell–sprayed hairdo frizzing in the humidity. The sound of traffic would be muffled, an occasional unorchestrated popping of it with a lift of wind through the shop door. My mom would be blankly staring toward the street, a domesticated version of the thousand-yard stare as she surveyed her outer world without moving an eye so much, as if the world itself, the way a soldier sees it, the way my brother saw it, the way my sister saw it on Bourbon Street, were a memory of violence.

MY SISTER STANDS in her doorway, waiting for me to get out of my car, her long hair concealed beneath a baseball cap. When I meet her on the porch of this $500,000 home, I hug her and wonder if she shuts herself in every day, shades drawn against the light. The truth is that I just don't know very much about my sister's life anymore, which saddens me, and the sadness paints the way I see her with a grim, grey-colored brush. I want that to stop, like so many other things I want stopped in my life. I want to remember my sister as the girl again, whom I protected from lascivious solicitors when I was only thirteen and she was seventeen, laughing at my rebukes of people she saw to be relatively innocent passersby. Construction workers whistled; men at the mall threw gazes her way while walking with their wives. I flipped them all the bird and was always ready to fight if it came to that—which it never did—all 105 pounds of me at that time twitching with hostility but relatively inept.

About twenty minutes after showing up at her house, my sister and I go to an AA meeting together in a neglected retail space—the same AA meeting my father will later belittle us for attending. Not everybody goes to these meetings for the same reasons. We have our own reasons, my sister and I, and they have nothing to do with alcohol. My sister cries during the meeting. My own eyes water up. Both of us might be meant for this room, even if not entirely bonded by the same disease as the others.

We've been sitting in metal card chairs around a banquet table. My sister's purse is on the ground, and when we stand up to leave, she briefly stumbles over it. She holds on to the table the way you hold on to the railing of a boat when it's going over a wave, and I remember her at the funeral and think: *Grief again,* but I don't know why.

I don't know how I got this way, why this is my world instead of other, more bountiful ones, but when I see my sister I know that I am not alone. I wonder if I could die in this house I've built around my suffering, waiting for my sister to come home to me so we can soften the pain together.

There's a big part of me that realizes, I guess, that if my hunt through this case isn't only about the crimes—if this story is also about me—I'll still have to follow the blood.

PSYCHIC

I'm sitting at the Stillwater Grill in Okemos, interviewing Erica and her father again, when they tell me about their experience with the television psychic John Edward. In October of 2009, Tom Ascroft, Erica, and Tom's niece went to Cobo Hall in Detroit, where three hundred people had crowded inside a ballroom to see John Edward in action as he affirmed their links to the dead and the longed-for.

"The Edward routine goes like this," Erica tells me, tapping out an ellipsis with her forefinger before continuing. "Guests fill up the chairs surrounding him, and then John Edward walks around and gets hits on people related to his psychic impressions of them. Or he gets no hit on you, depending. If he does get a hit, he tells you what it's about."

She continues, "He comes up and he tells us— and the whole place is looking, you know—and he says, 'This is really weird, but who had the pet monkey?' "

Erica's father interrupts her story, laughing, his eyes widening when he says to me, "So my niece stands up and she says, 'Oh my God, my grandmother had a monkey when I was in Pennsylvania.' "

They're all very impressed by this, but at the end of the day it's just a monkey until John Edward says, "Hold on." And then he points to Erica and her father and says, "Would you please get up and separate from the group?"

So they stand up and they move to some empty seats, Erica says. They're isolated and it feels awkward.

John Edward says, "There is so much going on around you." And then he adds, "One of you has lost a contemporary." John Edward clarifies that, by contemporary, he means someone of not just proximity in age but of the same bloodline.

Erica says to him, "I did."

And then John Edward says, "There was a crime committed. There's something about bite marks. There's a suitcase with film. There's videotapes and pictures in it. And there's something about bloody ropes."

I'm impressed but also skeptical. It's possible that John Edward has a team of researchers, that the producers preinterview the guests, that the information is just out there and that maybe he uses an email address, or a name on the credit card used to buy tickets, or anything else to find out information beforehand.

And so I ask Erica, "Could he have read about all of this somewhere?"

Erica and her father look at me. Both of them laugh. "Nobody knew about any of this," she tells me, "until he said it at Cobo."

"But *you* knew it," I suggest. "We've talked about all of this. Maybe he has a team working for him."

"We *didn't* know it," Erica says. "That's the whole fucking point. But every one of the things he said turned out to be true."

What she's telling me is that John Edward, the psychic, knew about Christopher Busch before anybody outside of the police had associated him with the OCCK murders.

"We're still looking for the bite marks," Erica's father says. "But the suitcase and all that shit, nobody outside of the PD knew this until we went to that show, and then we started looking into it more."

Erica looks at her father first, then at me, and says, "And he specifically said to us, after describing it all, 'You're going to be opening Pandora's box very soon. Whatever this crime was, you're closing in on resolution.' "

ERICA AND KRISTINE'S mother, Debbie Jarvis (formerly Mihelich and Ascroft), had been hands-off for decades, unable to talk about her oldest daughter's murder, and had been in spotty communication with Erica around 2009. The day after the John Edward experience, however, Erica's mother called her out of the blue, not knowing about their psychic consultation, as Debbie and Tom had been divorced for years. She asked Erica to accompany her to see a Detective Garry Gray, one of the original task force members in 1977, who'd also eventually traveled with Cory Williams to Atlanta.

She'd felt something inside, a voice, telling her to become involved in the case once again. She didn't know why, but she'd decided to listen.

Later that week, Erica and her mother visited Detective Gray. It was the first time in Erica's life that she'd spoken with anybody in an official capacity about the case. She was five when Kristine was murdered and nobody from the PD, or even local cops, had ever interviewed her. The press had never bothered her, either.

When they sat down in Detective Gray's office, she saw, set to the side on his table, a three-ring case binder with three names highlighted on the cover of it: Christopher Busch, Vince Gunnels, and Gregory Greene.

Names that neither Erica nor anyone outside of the police had heard of in relationship to the OCCK case, until this point in 2009, over thirty years later.

When Erica asked Detective Gray about the binder, he paid her lip service by flipping through it, mentioning the three names as persons of interest but allowing only a cursory examination of the paperwork inside. When Gray came to a photograph of the Christopher Busch suicide scene, he attempted to cover it from view with his hand but Erica grabbed the binder from him and turned it toward herself.

Against Gray's will, Erica and her mother looked at the photograph, which depicted a body laid out in a bed, presumably Christopher Busch's. His head was covered by a sheet, which was covering the reported gunshot wound as well. That the photograph would be taken after covering the wound seemed counterintuitive to me.

And they flipped through other photographs as well, she tells me, absorbing a new world of information, an opening into the case.

Tacked above Christopher Busch's bedroom dresser: a pencil sketch of what looked to be victim #1, Mark Stebbins.

On the closet floor: the suitcases.

On the bedroom floor: the set of bloody ligatures.

When Erica asked Detective Gray about the ligatures, he said, "That's where it gets a little tricky."

He told her that the ligatures found in Busch's Bloomfield home, similar to the ligatures found at the family cabin in Ess Lake, had been "lost."

If Christopher Busch killed himself, he did so after setting out evidence that would link him to the crimes—the ropes, the suitcase, possibly the drawing of Mark Stebbins.

Erica sat back in her chair, realizing that John Edward had been right: the ligatures, the suitcase of pornography—evidence on the books for decades, and nobody had told the families of the victims.

THERE ARE TWO different narrative reports of the Christopher Busch suicide, one of them saying that a .22-caliber rifle was "by [Busch's] side" and the other saying that the rifle was "pointing at his head" when it was found. Either way, we know there was a .22 rifle present. Both reports conclude that Busch shot himself with this rifle, and yet five different cotton swabs of Christopher Busch's hands showed no gunshot residue.

H. Lee Busch, upon being notified of his son's demise, returned from Europe. For some reason he was allowed to keep the .22-caliber rifle, the reported instrument of death, in his possession for over a month. The police had him sign a hand-written promissory note saying that he would return the weapon as evidence when convenience allowed.

Just days after Christopher Busch's death, the OCCK Task Force, comprising hundreds of investigators in multiple jurisdictions, disbanded for reasons that were cited as financial.

They claimed they'd been drained of resources.
No more OCCK killings occurred after that.

I'M LOOKING OVER the Christopher Busch suicide papers at a diner. They seem thin for such a high-profile suspect. I'm supposed to meet Ellie again in a few hours. I slide my coffee aside and take out a few of the massive case files from my bag. I place them on the table in front of me and when I dig into them I'm searching for commonalities in suspects.

Right before I realize I'm running late for Ellie, it finally occurs to me that every suspect file, every crime scene report, and every statement from a witness has the appropriate police department stamp at the top with an officer as signatory at the bottom.

The police themselves are the only commonality, and yet so obvious a link hadn't crossed my mind until now, years into my investigation. Like Cathy's father, I've been giving law enforcement the benefit of the doubt because I generally believe in the sanctity of our institutions. However, it's that same belief system—our blind acceptance of the authority of a badge—that allows a young boy to get into an unmarked car with a man in uniform, if for no other reason than because he's been told to.

When I think about this, I get angry, like Cathy, who emails me statements like "These pussies don't know who they're fucking with now."

None of us has forever. Sometimes our obsessions *are* the truth. All we have time for is to follow their paths, to look into a crowd and think, like the psychic, *What am I getting a hit on here?*

THE HAUNTING

There are large gaps in time.

Or there are no gaps in time, and today I am as close to 1976 and 1977 as I am to whatever happened in my life this very week. I see photos of myself as a young boy and photos of my children at that same age, all spread atop the table in front of me, and there is nothing to tell me that time has passed between the taking of an older photo and a newer one.

There is set dressing to indicate change—a chair and a card table from thirty years ago, and now a vase with an old flower in it from 2009, everything exactly where it should be—but I am the same in each photo, the ones of myself and the ones of my children, whom I see my features in. I am in there with them.

Now, in January of 2012, it has been fourteen months since I last saw Ellie, which means it's been fourteen months since I was last in Detroit, although it feels like weeks or minutes ago. Here in Idaho, the weather is a balmy forty degrees. My wife and I, now separated, are sharing the kids one week on, one week off. This week I'm alone, and there's a sinking in my gut that started the moment I dropped the kids at her house yesterday. Things haven't gotten better, the way people said they would—they've gotten lower and wider inside, without my kids.

Over the previous year, we'd spent months falling apart, even after I came home. At night, on the long, L-shaped couch we'd raised our kids on and that I'd taken to sleeping on, I'd run the case through my head, falling asleep only in fits. The streetlight outside our living room windows would slant across my body.

Sometimes I'd see the headlights of our various neighbors swinging around the corner at odd hours. I'd hear the guy across the street pulling into his carport some nights. I didn't know it yet, but he'd been coming home from hiding out with my wife.

Lying there, images of eleven-year-old Timothy King at his drop location would begin to haunt me: laid onto his stomach in the snowy ditch, his face smooshed sideways, his lips parting slightly as if drooling onto a pillow. I'd thought for a long year that he'd been deposited neatly, tucked in like a teddy bear off Gill Road that night in 1977. Hundreds of news articles I'd read had led me to believe this, but those articles had been a misdirect, like so many other things I'd thought about the case.

Timothy King, contrary to those articles, lay

twisted onto himself in the crime scene photos, a broken body, washed in the photographer's light.

When my wife's car arrived home one night in late summer, only a minute before the neighbor's car swooped into his own driveway, something in me clicked and I began to understand that they'd been having an affair.

It took me three months to prove.

First I asked my wife about it, and she denied everything. I told her that I wanted honesty in our lives. She told me that all of this "searching for criminals" had made me crazy.

She said I needed psychiatric help. She said, "You can't keep thinking everybody is lying to you."

The neighbor's daughter and my son were in the same class that year. At the Back to School Picnic at the end of August, my wife and the neighbor took special pains to avoid one another so as not to alert me. I watched the guy crack jokes in a corner of the playground, his smile so greasy you could simmer fries in it. The heat in me rose but I stayed quiet, wanting to save my kids from the heartache of divorce.

WHEN MY WIFE and I were finally over, I cried into the empty rooms of our house, which we put on the market. I eventually lost my car and job, as I was mentally unable to work. Soon I was forced to sell most of my possessions. Very few of my friends called to check on me. Eventually my wife and I began living in rented homes and I got on with my life, but only in five-minute intervals that felt stretched and darkened across my eyes.

Later I spent long evenings on the edge of violence, wanting to corner my wife's new lover, the man who'd been living within eyeshot of my children, within eyeshot of the couch I'd been sleeping on those nights before everything fell apart.

Most people don't know the kind of violence that takes over a heart in situations like that. Whatever your endgame was for your life, it changes without notice on you. The endgame is now, you realize, and that's all you can see. You're suddenly a silhouette standing in an open street, holding a weapon in the darkness, until a set of headlights swings around and drapes you, locks you in their net of light, and you see yourself for who you are. You see yourself as they do.

There were times when I'd call Cathy Broad, needing somebody who understood in me what my wife couldn't, how a haunting takes over, how when you look in the mirror after a while all you can see is this unnamed thing that's darker than you, that got inside.

Cathy told me that people were reading her emails and texts, that there was a ghost in the machine. I'd been feeling the same for months, watching the cursor on my laptop move some-times, with seemingly no one at the controls. One afternoon I got into my car and realized that somebody had been riffling through it.

I stepped out the driver's-side door and looked under the oil pan. I popped the hood and stared at the battery. When I got home that evening, there was a light on over my sink that I hadn't turned on.

MARK STEBBINS

M ark Stebbins was the first victim of the Oakland County Child Killer. He was twelve years old. On February 15, 1976, he was at a work-related party with his mother at the American Legion Hall in blue-collar Ferndale, where the buildings are mostly brick and the streets turn grey from slush in the wintertime.

It was midafternoon, the day after Valentine's Day.

Mark Stebbins left the hall and began a short walk to his home, supposedly to watch a movie on television instead of hanging out with his mom, who stayed behind and didn't return home until evening to check on him.

Four days later Mark Stebbins was found in the parking lot of a small strip mall in Southfield, just up the road from a Michigan State Police outpost and about two miles from my own boyhood home. His body had reportedly been laid atop a low brick wall bordering the rear of the lot. Along with the double-barrel-shaped imprint on his head, a postmortem report showed Mark Stebbins had been sexually penetrated and his wrists and ankles showed ligature marks, although none of that information was released to the public.

At the Christopher Busch crime scene, where Busch had been found dead in his bedroom, a pencil drawing of a boy found tacked to his wall showed a great likeness to the Mark Stebbins publicity sketch previously released to the press in an effort to help with their search during the boy's captivity period. In the Busch sketch, however, Stebbins is wearing a hooded sweatshirt pulled up over his hair, his eyes closed, his face screaming out in pain.

The sketch found at the Busch residence was concealed from the press and the Stebbins family, as well as from the families of the three other OCCK victims, even though there were many in law enforcement who presumed the sketch to implicate Busch in at least the murder of the Stebbins boy. Busch, they believed, had sketched the young boy as he'd looked in captivity, then showcased the drawing as a memento.

There were two officers at the Busch suicide scene, a flurry of investigators afterward, and countless other cops over the decades who had looked through the files. Outside their own ranks, they were silent about the drawing.

There are questions surrounding the sketch's placement at the scene, however. While some take it at face value, to have been drawn by

Busch, it may also have been planted there after his death. Adding to the mystery of the sketch is that, decades after his alleged suicide, one of Busch's nephews claimed to have seen the sketch in Busch's bedroom months before the Stebbins abduction even occurred. If the nephew is to be believed, the Stebbins likeness might be a coincidence, a sketch of another boy somehow, or it might be a foreshadowing of the Stebbins abduction: Busch may have somehow known Stebbins prior to abducting him and sketched out the look on his face as he fantasized about it.

Busch could have held on to the sketch for a period prior to the murder, then played out the scene in real life. Alternatively, the nephew could be lying about having seen the sketch earlier, hoping to deflect law enforcement's interest in the family line.

When considering the pencil sketch, however, it should be taken into account that Busch had no genuine artistic skills and that the likeness, which is very astute, even if coincidental, likely could not have been drawn by Busch in the first place.

The pencil sketch in question, then, was either gifted to Busch by an associate or planted in his bedroom after the supposed suicide. Busch did not draw the boy—that much can be assumed with accuracy. He simply didn't have the talent for it.

EYEGLASSES

I'd been talking on the phone to Ellie about her recovery, almost daily, from the porch of our home in Idaho. It freaked me out that she'd survived her addictions and come out ahead. That hadn't seemed in the cards for Ellie, not ever. Now she seemed so honest with herself— and honest with me about my own problems, too. She'd been teaching me to forgive myself for whatever darkness I carried.

Talking to Ellie felt right at the time, and I saw nothing about that as a violation of morality, as a transgression. In retrospect, I was blinded and propelled. No better than my wife in those moments. But we often only learn these lessons in reverse proportion to their usefulness.

What I did see, in moments of clarity and calmness, was that with Ellie's help I'd become a better person on the whole. Even though my life at home was falling to pieces, I'd thought I was falling in love again, surprised at being capable of such a thing after living so long without real connection to anyone other than my kids. Sometimes I worried that we'd all inevitably end up like the OCCK victims, either discarded or simply alone. I fought against that feeling by latching onto Ellie, imagining us together somehow: Ellie a companion to my darkness, someone to hold my hand through the loneliness.

But I'd been confusing intimacy with love. It had been so long since I'd opened myself to anybody. So many years had gone by since I'd allowed myself to be vulnerable that I didn't understand how human connection and romantic love were two different things.

So when Ellie stopped calling me out of the blue, the same year that I'd eventually discover my wife's affair, it was like I'd been drugged, then placed on a table and cut into quarters for wrapping, one piece of me over here, another over there, my center point—an anxiously beating heart—set adrift without oars to guide it. One day everything had been ordinary and dependable, and the next day Ellie was a ghost. She—a person I'd come to depend on—wouldn't answer her phone and wouldn't respond to texts.

I tried for months to get in touch with her and couldn't—months I spent in a daze, not so much depressed as numb. I withdrew from my life and the few friends I had, even withdrew from my children.

I made very little impression on my class at the university and eventually quit teaching without consulting with my wife. We'd soon be poor again, but I couldn't care about that. All I could think about was that Ellie must have been using again, that she'd slipped away into whatever drugs she'd stumbled onto at the very right moment for them to take hold, because that's how a relapse happens.

And maybe I had relapsed, too, but in a different way. I'd been trying so hard to become somebody I could respect and yet I'd let myself get jacked up by Ellie once again, just like I had during our first go-together. I'd asked her to marry me back in our twenties but instead of saying yes she'd broken up with me, confessing to coking out and screwing a bassist in a punk band nearly every day of the entire month that I'd been planning our vows.

Now I'd been choosing to replace the impending loss of my marriage with a woman who I must have known would abandon me over and over, no matter how hard I tried to prevent that from happening. It was what I'd looked for my whole life, since my father had stopped showing up on visiting days when I was a boy: for that pain to keep repeating itself.

Ellie disappearing on me again was everything I'd ever asked of the world.

I WAS STANDING in the airport in Detroit, having arrived to continue my investigation. I waited for my duffel in the terminal and checked my phone to find a friend request from Ellie on

Facebook. She must have known I was coming back. A few independent news articles had come out online, and maybe she'd read about my continued work on the case.

For a moment I imagined accepting her friend request, exchanging a few messages with her, getting resolution over coffee, falling in love again, starting the whole thing over like I'd never learned a lesson in my life. It would have been so easy.

The baggage carousel circled. I felt stupid. I felt young and dumb and pulsing with want for her. I ignored her friend request, grabbed my bag, and texted my father, who'd been circling the airport in a rental car he'd put on his credit card for me while waiting for my plane to arrive.

I walked outside into the humidity and stood near the taxi lane. My father texted me three more times because he'd been circling the wrong terminal. Eventually he called.

"Where the fuck are you?" he said.

A few more minutes later I got into the car. We shook hands.

"Those are some ugly fucking glasses," he told me while puffing out steam, frustrated after getting lost. I took my glasses off, put them in their case. I checked my phone for messages again. I checked my emails. Ignored the friend request.

My father and I barely spoke as he drove.

192

HUG YOUR MOM GOOD-BYE

My dad took me back to his house for dinner right after picking me up at the airport. My dad's new wife, his third, was there to greet me with a Crock-Pot full of sausage and kale. She was my age, studying to get into a nursing school in Detroit, and they'd been married for five years.

She smiled a lot during dinner.

We ate the sausage and kale out of bowls, sitting at their small table in the galley-style kitchen. My dad had come around since his car-ride silence, asking me questions about the case. They had three cats and I'm allergic, so I tried not to touch the tabletop while I ate. My father was also allergic but took an antihistamine every day. The cats were his wife's. When he'd met her, he'd had to make a decision about that.

After dinner, I went into my dad's little office with him to look at his stuff. On the shelves sat pictures of his kids, books, old feathers in a small basket, the photo of my sister when she was in high school, wearing her boyfriend's varsity jacket and my dad's cowboy hat as a lark. The glass on that picture frame had gone dusty.

"I had more books," my dad said. "But I got rid of them."

Where the books used to be was a row of pill bottles. He'd been suffering from joint pain for a few years and had heart issues but never talked openly about his health or body. Underneath his abrasive exterior was an uncharacteristic modesty in matters of the flesh. I was in college before I'd seen him without a shirt on, for instance. I'd come to visit him without advance notice and found him sunbathing in the backyard in the middle of a workday. He'd seemed annoyed, maybe at getting caught loafing, but my feeling at the time was that he'd been embarrassed at his body having gone soft over the years, a body that, until then, I'd childishly viewed as more wood and stone than human and perishable.

A part of me was excited at the chance to figure out my dad again during this trip, thinking that maybe he'd surprise me. The other part of me, the part that never knew him without having to guess, still felt slighted at the extent of what he'd show of himself: a few trinkets, some old photos meant to explain his passions, a regimen of plastic pill bottles indicating how much time he had left.

Looking at my dad's stuff, I made a mental note to study the Christopher Busch "suicide" photos. Snapped in his bedroom, the clutter might tell me as much as his DNA. What books had he read?

What medications had he taken that kept him awake, or put him to sleep? Who had he been after all? What would Christopher Busch let me see?

My dad and I made plans for breakfast in a few days. He joked, "Hug your mom good-bye." I looked at his wife and blushed.

I'M IN DETROIT for six weeks. It won't be enough time to learn what I want, so I start quickly. In the mornings I go to the public library to check their microfilm, looking for relevant news articles from the first of the killings until after Christopher Busch's death. It's approximately a two-year span.

I bring in a coffee from the Starbucks that first morning and sit in the viewing room in the dark, scrolling through film. I go month by month, and it takes two hours before I stumble onto a photograph of a gold-colored two-door Mercedes that'd been car bombed.

In the photo, a detective stands in the background, trench-coated to his knees. It's cold outside. His hands are in his pockets. His face is shriveled. His foot is frozen in the frame, a single black wingtip kissing at shrapnel on the ground, blasted out from the console in a spray of what'd become ashen already by the time of the photo.

Short of a half dozen articles on child molestations by priests, which I send to the printer, nothing else stands out that I hadn't already seen online in the past two years or received from Cathy. I make a note to get the case report on the car bombing.

I doze in the darkness, and when I open my eyes again, I put my hand on the machine and I can feel it hum, the years passing away from me but in reverse, on hot cellulose and without color.

It's late afternoon by the time I leave the library. I have dinner plans with an old friend but not until eight o'clock. I have a good three hours to kill, so I drive into the city, taking Woodward Avenue instead of the freeway. I pass through Highland Park, the burned-out retail shops, a few of them still smoldering from recent arsons.

I park near the Detroit River. There's a ferry-boat anchored. I get out of my car and a breeze off the well-oiled marina cools my skin. It feels good. I sit on a park bench across from two black men, both around fifty and eating chicken out of a bag. They nod at me. I nod back. One of them says, "You want one of these legs?" but he's just fucking with me. I think, *Idaho could use a few characters like these.* I can see myself moving back to Detroit one day, if only to be around the variety of personalities and cultures again, that grit and vibrancy. Ellie would be here, too, though, and that would be a problem for me if I were trying to stay healthy.

I stare across the river to Windsor, in Canada. It's close enough to be just another part of Detroit, but after homeland security became an issue, you need a passport to get there. Windsor's about a ten-minute drive through the tunnel, including checkpoints, a little longer if you take the bridge.

I call my sister and leave a message that I know she won't return. I doze on the bench for an hour, and when I sit up finally, the two guys are gone and I'm alone by the water. I think about Teresa, the woman I'm meeting for dinner. I saw her once for a brief coffee last fall, the day I was leaving Detroit for Idaho, but I'd been distracted that day and we'd barely gotten a chance to talk.

Before that, we hadn't seen each other in twelve years. My daughter had been three years old the last time we spoke. Teresa and I had met in the afternoon, and I'd felt ambushed by her dirty-blond, almost brown hair thinned by sunlight streaming into the bar. We'd drunk a few beers and then walked to a train tracks nearby. Teresa had taken my hand, and we'd pressed our backs against a retaining wall.

"In a few minutes, the train will come by," she'd said. "Don't move."

I'd stood with my back to the wall, slightly buzzed, holding Teresa's hand for the first time. We'd known each other since we were eleven. I'd always liked her.

The train had roared by three feet in front of us. I'd felt my cheeks quiver. I haven't felt beautiful like that in a long time.

THIS TRIP, I meet Teresa at Anita's Kitchen in Ferndale. It's a Mediterranean place on Woodward Avenue with outdoor seating. Teresa's early, sitting at a table outside, wearing gold-tinted aviator glasses when I arrive, also early. She's checking her phone, her long, straight hair hugging her jawline while she looks at the messages in her lap. When she looks up at me approaching, I blush a little.

We hug. She feels good.

We spend three hours eating and catching up. Teresa tells me about the "nickel" she'd spent hanging out with bands like the White Stripes in the Detroit music scene, the five years she'd spent renting a room in a home down the block from crack houses.

She tells me about the neighbors who'd gotten broken into twice in one month before buying a pit bull as protection.

"A week later, somebody broke in again, only this time they stole the pit bull," she says, laughing.

We don't leave Anita's until they make us leave. Dipping in and out of my conversation with Teresa are thoughts of Ellie and my wife, but I'm compartmentalizing, telling myself that one thing is not affected by the other. I am wrong, of course, but I don't know that yet. Teresa gets a carryout container, slides in whatever food we have left, and then hands it to me on the way out.

"You look like you could use it," she says.

I walk Teresa to her car. The air is humid and thick in the streetlights. We stand next to her car door and the moment is suspended. She has a boyfriend. I have kids.

I hug her good-bye.

On the car ride home a few minutes later, I get a text from her.

It's good knowing you're around, it says.

THE WOMAN IN THE TRANSCRIPT

I'm sitting on the bed in my hotel after returning from dinner, staring at a faxed transcript, nineteen pages of testimony to the FBI, given in 1992 by a now-grown female victim of heinous multiple molestations. The television is on mute and I've avoided calling home.

In the transcript, the victim states that she and her sister witnessed the murder of a small boy, approximately five to eight years old, with blond curly hair. The boy knelt on the ground while the girls watched their father strike him in the head with a baseball bat. The boy was unknown to them. Her father and another man present discussed what to do with the boy's body.

The woman in the transcript describes another homicide, of a nine-year-old female, occurring in what the woman described as a doctor's office of sorts. The nine-year-old lay on an examination table. She had long, dark hair. She was molested on the table by a man who stabbed her in the stomach afterward. The nine-year-old fell off the table. Again there was discussion about what to do with the body.

The woman in the transcript states that she believes her father to have been involved in a pedophile ring and that her father recruited members from St. Joseph Catholic Church in Dexter, Michigan. She states that the ringleader was not her father but a prominent and powerful person in the Ann Arbor community a few miles away, where Frank Shelden lived before fleeing the country. She describes the man as having a beard and dark hair and as being very large.

Shelden didn't look that way. Christopher Busch looked exactly that way, though. He was bearded and weighed 250 pounds at the time of his death, and children get confused.

The woman in the transcript states that a doctor from Dexter, Michigan, performed an abortion on her sister, who was pregnant due to incest. The woman in the transcript was forced to watch this abortion being performed so that she would recognize the seriousness of the procedure and avoid becoming pregnant.

The woman had a brother who was also questioned by the FBI. He stated that both sisters were indeed molested and that those molestations had been photographed. He had several photographs in his possession, presumably having kept them over the years as evidence.

The woman in the transcript states to the FBI

that when the pedophile ring came together, they would usually occupy a shed near a gravel pit in Dexter. Gregory Greene had stated himself, in testimony before his sentencing on the molestation charges, that he and Busch would exchange children at an isolated, nondescript gravel pit that they both had easy access to.

The woman will refuse any interviews by the cops working in Dexter, or by any other Detroit-area police personnel, she says, as she feels that during the time of her own abuse, occurring from 1975 to 1976, several local police officers were somehow involved.

She states that when she was six years old she was made to have sex with men in her living room while her father watched. Often there were "parties" attended by other prepubescent girls and other old men alongside them.

The woman in the transcript states that she and her sister were driven to a two-story office building in Ann Arbor, where they were taken into a white room and photographed together. She said this happened approximately twice a year for four years, and that other men occasionally showed up for photographic sessions with other girls. The photographer was always the same photographer, she said.

WHEN I GET out of the hotel shower the next morning, there's a phone message from my sister.

She wants to see me, she says, but today she's busy. She wants to see me tomorrow instead.

I call her back. She doesn't answer my call and her voice mail is full. I drive to her neighborhood, eat breakfast for two dollars in a diner, then sit in my car down the block from her house and call her again. She doesn't answer but texts me that she's busy. I can see her car in the driveway, a black Mercedes.

The next day I get back on the freeway and eventually sit inside a Dunkin' Donuts near my hotel, going over the Fox Island files I've brought along in my computer bag to link-chart the pornography syndicate. There's a photocopied bank check accompanied by a receipt from a hotel restaurant in Port Huron. The bill was for sixteen dollars, paid for by the William Angell Foundation, as noted on the check. I push the photocopies around on the table in front of me, stare at them while I eat a donut.

I do a little research, pirating a wireless connection, and find that William Angell had been the president of Continental Motors, a defunct automobile engine manufacturer that turned to producing aircraft engines, previously headquartered in Muskegon, Michigan, where suspects Christopher Busch, Frank Shelden, and John all had occasionally spent time in the summers. An ancestor of his, James Burrill Angell, had been the third president of the University of Michigan and the longest serving, spanning thirty-eight years from 1871 to 1909.

The William R. Angell Foundation, established to provide scholarships in biology, had also owned North Manitou Island, a stone's throw from the Fox Island porn ring. The foundation had sold the property to the National Park Service in 1984, the same period that Fox was sold off.

THE NEXT DAY I drive over to rural Dexter, an hour from my hotel, to find what I believe to be the gravel pit mentioned by the woman in the FBI transcript.

There are many gravel pits, of course, but this particular one had been frequented by earth science classes in the 1960s and 1970s on field trips to explore the natural habitat and varied geological ecosystems. As gravel pits go, it was a known meeting point.

Once called the Whittaker-Gooding pit, the land was purchased by Mel and Betty Fox in 1973. Mel Fox was an entrepreneur in the medical industries, which interests me because many of the wealthier of the Angells' ancestors were in the medical field, and the FBI transcripts also mention a medical office where the girl witnessed the multiple sex crimes and possible murders.

I don't yet know if Mel and Betty's last name is related to the Fox Islands. All I have are my notes and a hunch, but I do know that the land, which is sprawling, is now named the Fox Science Preserve.

I also know, more importantly, that this might be the only gravel pit that makes sense. Suspects Greene and Busch could possibly have been here as kids.

As I drive down the rural road toward the gravel pit, I remember being at a winter camp with my school: I'm about eight years old and we're there to cross-country ski and snowshoe, build survival shelters, and study the winter stars through telescopes. We stay in cabins for three days. Our chaperone is a volunteer, about nineteen years old. In my cabin, it's me and about ten other boys from my class. One of them, a boy named Aaron, has hearing aids.

We're all wearing long underwear, preparing a skit for the final night's talent show, and Aaron keeps messing up his lines. The chaperone is frustrated with him. Aaron laughs at something, I don't remember what, and the chaperone side-kicks him in the stomach, sending Aaron, a seventy-pound half-deaf kid, across the floor and into a wall.

Aaron starts to cry. Time stops. Then the chaperone says to all of us, "You better not tell anybody I did that."

And so we don't.

PLACEMENT

I'm waiting for my lunch at a Coney Island restaurant that backs up to the parking lot where victim #1, Mark Stebbins, was found. I've ordered a Coney dog and a Diet Coke.

I've just come from walking off a path the Oakland County Child Killer might have taken before placing Mark Stebbins's body on the brick wall outside, a hundred yards away. I held my Flip cam while walking the perimeter.

A slight mist fell on me, the clouds having gone grey in a way most Detroiters recognize. A man came out of a hat store, watched me pace off the distance from a Dumpster to a wall. He smoked a cigarette.

Later on, in my playback, he looks a little like Detroit-area champion boxer Thomas Hearns, my father's hero, skinny and angular in the frame.

I'VE BEEN BOTHERED lately by the placement of the bodies, all of them in public locations, viewable but only from particular angles. Passersby could see them, surely, but not *all* passersby. The bodies were either placed strategically or simply dumped as fast and near as convenience would allow.

Was it a coincidence that both Mark and Jill were deposited within shooting range of the Michigan State Police and the Troy Police Departments, respectively? It's possible that the drop locations were indeed random, of course: whatever was easiest at the time. In the Stebbins case, his drop was only a handful of miles from the abduction site. It's entirely possible that the OCCK took a regular route through that area for unrelated business. Stebbins, possibly kept nearby during captivity, was perhaps unloaded hard and fast from the killer's vehicle, which may have been backed up to that wall.

The press said the killer was taunting the police, but maybe he was actually caring for the victims by getting them back to their homes faster, placing them in a location readily discoverable. Had he felt that he'd been tucking them safely back into their world again, their purpose already served?

I'M HAVING BREAKFAST with my dad the next day, in a diner at seven a.m. at the corner of 9 Mile and Southfield Road, across from Southfield High School. My dad's been flirting with the waitress, predictably. She's maybe twenty years old, fifty years his junior. He's sucking on a toothpick that he'd pulled from behind his ear.

He makes fun of the way I'm eating my bacon, picking off the rubbery fat with my fingertips, eating only the meat.

He says, "Bacon is good because it's fucking fat, you asshole."

He gets quiet after I don't respond. He tells me that he wasn't a great dad, but he's old now, he says, and because of this he has a lot to offer.

"Advice on eating bacon," I say.

"Look," he says. He pushes his coffee. "You got a chip on your shoulder."

"I'm just here to have breakfast and you're calling me an asshole."

After a while he says, "It takes somebody like you to find this killer. You've got real balls going after this guy."

Then he says, "Let me ask you something. What makes you so interested in this?"

I don't answer him right away, because I'm thinking about the two cruisers who'd pulled behind him back in '77, how he'd watched the two cops get out with guns drawn, slinking toward both sides of his vehicle.

He sips his coffee then slides it aside and says, "Everybody has ghosts, you know."

Then he takes his toothpick and chews on it while I eat. When he pays our tab, he flirts with the waitress again.

"I have to come back here," I say. "Take it easy on her."

"Look," he says. "I didn't have much to offer, but what I did offer, you didn't take."

"Maybe," I tell him.

"Which way is north?" he says. He knows I've never learned these things. He's taking another jab at me.

I tell him, "Last winter, I got lost on one of those logging roads in the mountains, just out on a drive in the snow. It was stupid. I shouldn't have been out there. But you know what I did? I searched Google Maps on my iPhone. Then I drove where it told me to."

"Different generation," he says.

"Maybe," I tell him. "But I'm not hiking around Detroit with a compass and a canteen, for fuck's sake."

I eat my bacon and I tell him, "North is up."

ENDINGS

A lot of people related to the case have stayed in Michigan. Nearly all of the cops, nearly all of the family members of the victims, nearly all of the family members of the key suspects, and some of the key suspects themselves.

On my list of those who have left, however, are the two writers who came before me, attempting to understand this case in greater detail.

One of them, now a professor living out east who had moved his wife and small children to the Detroit area in '78 just after the murders ended, had a book deal in place with a publisher and, supposedly, open access to the police, but had left town within a year, taking with him the five hundred pages of a manuscript he said couldn't be finished.

I'd spoken with him on the telephone prior to my own investigation and he'd seemed unwilling to say much, or maybe I hadn't asked him the right questions.

"I haven't talked about this in a long time," he'd said.

"Why didn't you finish the book?" I'd asked him.

He'd hesitated, then told me, "There wasn't an ending."

THE OTHER WRITER, Tommy McIntyre, had been a reporter in the Detroit area during the 1970s and written a book called *Wolf in Sheep's Clothing: The Search for a Child Killer*, published in the late 1980s. People in Detroit know about the book, whose equally well-known cover features a rendering of the hockey-striped blue Gremlin allegedly driven by the suspected killer. The book itself, knowing what we now know, is outdated and favors the hard work of the police detectives whom McIntyre was friendly with. It draws no conclusions.

I'd had a hard time getting a line on McIntyre but finally pieced together that he'd recently stepped away from his job as a crime reporter for the local pamphlet-slash-paper in a small retirement community in Florida. He'd apparently left one of the most crime-ridden cities in America to spend his years reporting on shuffleboard arguments and stolen golf carts. It either made no sense at all or it made perfect sense.

When I'm in the Royal Oak library, waiting for my turn on the microfilm machine, I think about sending an email, but I don't even know what I'd say to McIntyre at this point. Even if he'd talk to me, I guess I'd only ask why he left. And even then, I think I'd already know the answer. The case is a scar on these writers' hearts, I imagine, thickened by shortcomings. I feel this way because I can feel my own scar thickening, lengthening across my chest. How many years have these writers lived with the brutality of this story in their minds, obsessing in the darker hours about its grimmest details?

How many years will I?

I check the microfilm for the art dealer John McKinney. I find two articles about his murder and one about a sex scandal of the same period involving a priest in Farmington. Then I find a fourth article, about a single-engine plane that went down over Lake Michigan.

Outside the library, I sit in my car and send emails from my phone. I text Cathy about meeting up with her father, who's planning on giving me more of the Freedom of Information Act documents, pages about the case I hadn't known existed.

I read an email from the assistant to John Walsh, the guy from *America's Most Wanted*, whose own son's abduction-murder in the 1980s prompted Walsh's work on these types of cases. We'd set up a phone call the week before, which he'd missed, and the assistant had emailed to set up another. She said she'd ping him a reminder this time.

I get a coffee and call Mark Wayno's home. Wayno's the boy whom the police had found riding his bicycle near the freeway, who'd lived down the street from the Stebbins family and gone missing but never spoken about it after he'd been found.

There's a woman's voice on an actual answering machine announcing the Wayno residence. I hang up without leaving a message, because even though I've been working this case for so long, I'm still tentative about interrupting lives. I'm hoping the voice belongs to Wayno's wife, though. When I think about it, I'm glad he has a family, a home telephone number. I'll be able to find him again if I need to, which is great, but it also feels good to know that he has a life in place when everything is stacked against so many others.

Maybe that's all I care about regarding Wayno. It seems like Wayno's story has an ending when so many of the other stories don't. There are so many starts and stops, like the writer who went home. It's frustrating, and yet, didn't I just do the same thing by hanging up on Wayno's answering machine? Am I failing myself, or are there parts of the story that I wasn't meant to know—that none of us were? Did those other writers know this, before I got here?

WHAT I'M DOING

I spend the morning in my hotel room skimming over the thousands of pages I'd copied out of Barry King's case files at a FedEx Office. I'm waiting for something to catch my eye. In the afternoon I go to a Starbucks on Orchard Lake Road in West Bloomfield. I get a coffee and I sit outside on the hood of my car. Across the parking lot, a plainclothes cop is leaning against his vehicle, watching me.

I text Cathy about it.

Take a picture of him, she texts back. **That always fucks them up.**

I hold my phone up and snap a picture of the cop. He stares at me a beat before getting into his car. He starts the engine, circles through the lot, and then parks about a hundred yards away, behind an SUV with clear windows that he can see through.

I get into my car and drive it closer to him, parking about four spaces away. I get out of my car again and walk back to the Starbucks and sit on a curb, sipping my coffee and watching the cop until he leaves. On his way out of the parking lot into traffic, he glances back at me.

Rabbit holes, I think. You can enter them, and never come out. Maybe I don't know what's real anymore.

I'm still at Starbucks, reading documents much later, when Cathy calls me to say that Kevin Dietz, a local reporter, will be on the six o'clock news announcing that a grand jury has been called in the OCCK case for the first time ever. In thirty-five years, nobody has attempted prosecution.

"What do they have?" I say.

"What *could* they have?" she says. "It's a fucking smoke screen. These scumbags have been lying for thirty-five years."

THAT NIGHT, I have dinner with Teresa. I'm sitting in a booth at another Middle Eastern restaurant, this time in Southfield, and I'm texting on my iPhone when she comes in and sits down looking beautiful and windswept.

We order. We talk about her boyfriend right away.

I ask her, "What are you doing?"

She sips from a Diet Coke, sets it aside, and says, "I don't know what I'm doing."

After a while I say, "If I'm interested in you, it's because I think I can learn from you. You're in a stable relationship. But that doesn't make sense if you're sitting here with me."

"It means I can be in one," she acknowledges.

I sip my own Diet Coke and then I say, "If I'm not interested in you, it's because you scare the shit out of me."

"You don't mince words," she tells me. "What could be so scary?"

"You getting found out," I say.

And then she says again, after a while, "I don't know what I'm doing, do I?"

We eat and she says, "I want to see you again."

I don't know what to think. We have so many years of history. The history that I've always wanted to build, that I'd been building with my family, but never with a woman separate from that. And yet I know that I am in the wrong, sitting here with her, taking away energy from my marriage and from Teresa's relationship with her boyfriend. I've done this before and know how it ends.

I drive back to my hotel after dinner and call my kids.

After I talk to them, I'm sitting on the edge of the bed and I want to get fucked up so bad. The TV is muted, the blue glow of it flickers against the room during a break from the Tot Mom trial. I want to hit something, put my elbow through the drywall, crack my head against the mirror. But I don't know why, and that part scares me as much as the wanting.

I put on my jeans and a hoodie and get into

216

my rental car and drive down 9 Mile, then cut into Detroit. It's dark out. I cruise past single-door taverns, a few prostitutes out front whom I slow down to watch. They're so alone on the streets. They were girls a long time ago; some of them probably still are, but in the glow of street-lamps they're on a stage when I drive by. They're staring back at me, into the lens of my window, and I feel like a creep.

I've been avoiding so much of the work I'm supposed to be doing for the case. I'm frozen up inside, afraid of maybe finishing, of burning out in failure. There's an incredible pain that keeps grinding deeper into my chest. Maybe it's the recognition of having spent so many years with my wife and still being alone somehow in the end. Maybe it's the nature of the work, like any work that takes you away from your children for lengthy periods. Or maybe it's the sadness that comes with acknowledging that my children, too, no matter how much love I give to them, may be hurting for more inside.

Maybe at the end of the day, I just want my father to have loved me properly back then, in a time that I can't return to, to make it right.

I pull over a few blocks from Comerica Park and I walk and put my hoodie up and stuff my hands into my pockets. It's hot out, and I'm sweating inside the cotton.

At some point I'm standing in front of my friend

Josh's building, staring up at it and wishing I would get shot in the head by a stranger, someone who would just say to me, "Look, man, you're done," and then butt his small pistol to the edge of my ear just under the hood of my sweatshirt.

I don't know how it would feel, if it would hurt for that second before I fell, but it can't hurt any worse than what I feel in this moment.

I am so alone, I am so alone, I keep thinking, and if it weren't for my children, I know that I would allow the indifference of this night to take hold.

And I am muted by those thoughts, and ashamed.

BLOOD, SEMEN, SALIVA, PRINTS

That night at three a.m., back on my hotel bed, I'm flipping through documents that might untie the ribbon on this case. Spread out on the bedsheets are dozens of pages that seem to irrefutably point to not only the cover-up of crime scene evidence but the intentional deflection toward a "lone killer" by the police in those early days.

According to what I've found, on February 20, 1976, evidence collected from the Mark Stebbins scene was received by Charlotte Day at the Michigan State Police crime lab and reported on March 2, 1976.

As chronicled in that report, on the body of Stebbins: his blue parka with bloodstains on the hood; blue jeans soiled with dirt and oil from the parking lot where he was found; trace fibers of white wool, red wool, blue wool, and yellow or gold carpeting; one human hair whose source was other than Stebbins; rodent hair and dog hair on all outerwear; an unknown source of decorative blue paint on Stebbins's left rubber boot; urine and fecal stains in his underpants; soil and perspiration stains on his T-shirt; bloodstains on the T-shirt; and Stebbins's red sweatshirt, stained by blood.

A subsequent report, prepared by Lourn Doan of the Southfield PD, states: "No blood in hair or clothes . . . indicating clothes and hair had been washed."

Lourn Doan's name shows up again at the top of a handwritten note, accompanied by the name of a Ferndale officer, Tom Cattle. Halfway down the note on the Stebbins evidence, it reads: "Sodomized. Sperm found in throat."

A supplemental report filed by the Livonia PD indicates that the autopsy of Stebbins, conducted by a Dr. Patanga, uncovered specimens of semen from both "the anal and oral cavities . . . Slides of the semen obtained from Dr. Patanga [were] transported to the Michigan State Police Crime Laboratory at Northville for blood type and secretion analysis."

The same report indicates that Stebbins was bound at the wrists and ankles by what was determined to have been "approximately 1/8" or 1/4" Bell Telephone Type wire."

A later report by the Michigan State Police indicates high levels of amylase, an enzyme found in saliva, on Stebbins's underpants, and another report indicates seventeen latent fingerprints on the body and clothing, none of which were his own.

Each report shows the cataloguing process and chain of custody of evidence associated with the Stebbins scene. Each report also shows this same cataloguing and chain of custody for additional fibers sampled from both a 1965 Pontiac and a 1965 Chevrolet (not a Gremlin), as well as fibers and other trace evidence from an unnamed suspect in relationship to that same vehicle.

This is in strong contrast to the public relations story about lack of evidence in the Stebbins case. To reiterate the stance of the police, ongoing since February of 1976, nothing was found on either the body or clothing of Mark Stebbins to indicate trace or hard evidence. According to public reports, the body and clothing had been meticulously scrubbed of any signs of the crimes committed against Stebbins during captivity and there was no reason to believe that the crimes were sexually motivated. All attention, according to police, should have been focused on profiling a lone serial killer of unknown motivation with both the highest intellect and intimate knowledge of criminology that would prompt him or her to finely scrub away any presence of physical intrusion upon the victim.

Compared to the actual case reports, it is easy to see that the truth of the Stebbins abduction and murder was quite the opposite of what police had advertised. There was nothing special about the Stebbins case, historically, other than the vast, improbable amounts of information being hidden, either in service to investigative efforts, as the police will have claimed, or, as I am increasingly assessing, in service to the continued obstruction of justice. Mark Stebbins was raped, murdered, and then dumped in plain sight—not by somebody taunting the police with the boldness of his body placement in that well-traveled retail district parking lot, but by somebody who just didn't give a fuck or know better.

Blood, semen, saliva, and fingerprints were found, Stebbins was filthy, and the PD who had a chance to bring this to light simply didn't.

They led us to look for an evil genius, but why?

DIAMOND EARRINGS.
SUGARLESS GUM.

Since I'm in Detroit, I meet up with my dad's second wife, Paula, for the first time in years, at a diner full of up-tempo Jews, movers and shakers mostly Paula's age, off Orchard Lake Road. A lot of diamond earrings in here, a lot of sugarless bubblegum cracking. Everybody uses a coupon, orders an omelet, talks about the trainers at their gym. Diners like this, with their Lexus-heavy parking lots, are all over the Bloomfield area, filled with the mothers of the wealthier kids I went to high school with, the ones who drove Corvettes, partied in hotel rooms, ran pyramid schemes, gambled on baseball games, and sold club drugs or started businesses by the time they were eighteen if they weren't going to law school or geared to become doctors.

Paula was the boss's daughter when my dad started working for the Mercury Paint Company in the mid-1970s. At the time, Mercury was a sixteen-store retail chain catering to house-painters, a behemoth in Detroit in the era prior to Home Depot. My dad had two master's degrees in psychology but in the end he'd stocked shelves and spent his days bullshitting with blue-collar workers, which he was more suited to. He'd had jobs working with kids in psychiatric wards like the now-closed Lafayette Clinic, but at some point my father had been fired and one of his uncles had gotten him the Mercury gig, which stuck.

Paula was ten years younger than my dad, came from money, and had an East Coast attitude that my mother simply couldn't compete with. The affair started when I was five. Paula would sometimes call the house, asking for my dad. My mother knew what was going on but couldn't stop it. She'd wear her bathrobe around the house and cry a lot.

I was ten when my dad and Paula married. Contrary to what I'd expected, Paula was warm and fun to be around. She smiled at me a lot, which my dad rarely did, and she'd gone to high school for a year with Madonna. She talked about New York, where one of her sisters was making a stab as a choreographer, and she took no bullshit on the phone in her business dealings, not from anybody.

I admired and was thankful for Paula, not for screwing over my mom, but for opening a door through which I vaguely sensed was a world bustling with people who'd managed to escape the fatigue of circumstance. My father probably felt the same way about her. Paula gave him an out, a chance to live extravagantly.

It's hot out when we meet, and I'm wearing cutoff army pants, a T-shirt, and two-dollar flip-flops. Paula tells me after we order, "You look like you're from California. You look relaxed."

"I feel fucked," I tell her.

"I know," she says. "But you don't look it."

She tells me she was at a party the night before and had met one of the assistant prosecutors for Oakland County. He'd given her his card to pass on to me but I know he was just being polite. None of these people will talk, not ever, not before or after grand juries convene—not even on their deathbeds, it seems, as plenty have slipped away without a word. I tell Paula I'll call him in a couple of weeks, after my kids have come and gone from a brief visit we'd planned in my despondency over leaving them.

She says, "Why wait to call the guy?"

I don't tell her that I've been getting emails from strangers, I've been in contact with some of the press in Detroit, and I've seen my name lambasted as a hack on some of the murder blogs around the Internet. I'm worried that the more often people learn of my presence here digging around, the more likely I am to find myself opening my hotel door to a .38 snub-nosed pistol pointed at my face. In a couple of weeks, after my kids have left, I'll reach into the danger zone,

225

and anybody with a beef can pop me if they want, but right now I am limiting my exposure.

What I also don't tell Paula is that the man she'd met, even if he's not super-comfortable on the grip end of a murder—even if he's just a plain, good guy—is among the least likely to provide new information. The prosecutor's office cultivates a shut-it-down mentality when it comes to controversy. There's no way some APA will open his heart, share a cup of coffee at Starbucks, and say, "You know who you ought to look at? The people who sign my checks."

TERESA CALLS ME when I'm on my way out of the hotel to get lunch the next day. She's in the parking lot with food for us, so I meet her in the lobby. We embrace for a long time, then separate.

Up in my room, we sit on my bed and eat. She's brought a loaf of French bread, some vegetables from her garden, some meats from a deli, and a Diet Coke for me. I pretend, for a while, that I am doing the right thing; but after we've eaten, the truth takes over. I know that I am spending time with Teresa for the very reasons my father left my mother for Paula: a hole in the world opened up and he was shown something he'd never have with my mom, and he walked through that hole and disappeared from us.

I think about my kids. I think about Teresa and whatever life she's built, the little I know of it.

"You've been with your boyfriend for ten years," I tell her.

"Maybe I'm not happy."

I don't tell her what I think: that nobody is fully happy, that every relationship on the planet is tainted by measures of unhappiness yanking at the seams of delight in them.

SLIDING WINDOWS

I spend a night wandering the downtown corridor on foot. I park outside the Lafayette Coney, get a hot dog with mustard and onions, and start walking, staying out of alleys.

I keep to the sidewalks and stroll. I pass Comerica Park where the Tigers play. A game is on, the stadium lights illuminating the block with spillover. The old baseball park from my youth, Tiger Stadium, is a dirt-covered lot now, cloaked by darkness a few miles away.

I pass a row of bars, hard-core rap shaking their foundations. Most of the streetlights are burned-out. A few people stare at me, but mostly nobody pays much attention. It feels good to disappear into the concrete.

It's hot out, maybe ninety degrees. I'm wearing my combat boots and jeans, a hoodie over my tank top. I tie the hoodie around my waist and sit on a curb near the river and I'm a small dot beneath the looming Renaissance towers where my high school buddies had rented rooms on Devil's Night to watch the city burn. I can see the lights of the Ambassador Bridge to Canada glowing in the distance, spanning the sheen of the river.

I get a text from Teresa that says she misses me today, wants to see me soon. I feel comforted by her, but I don't know how to process that. Comfort isn't the highs and lows of drama, not the thrill ride I'd grown up thinking love is.

Regardless, comfort and Teresa both seem like a distraction. I've come back to Detroit for the case, not to feel good about myself. So I don't text Teresa back that night. Walking back to my car, I pass the Joe Louis fist suspended in the median on Jefferson Avenue. I cross traffic and stand beneath it. I put my hand on the fist and let my fingers linger.

The next morning I wake up early, click my television to the Tot Mom trial, then put it on mute. I have breakfast in bed and make notes:

1. Where is the privately funded polygraph Busch supposedly failed (administered by Lawrence "Larry" Wasser)?
2. Talk to Lamborgine.
3. Talk to Vince Gunnels.
4. Call Dietz, Raj, and Hunt.
5. Name of the dry cleaners guy?
6. Talk to Gunnels' sister in Butte.
7. Talk to McKinney Jr.
8. Talk to Bridget.
9. John's sister works for Feiger!

10. Carl Leiter also represented CB alongside Burgess.
11. Reni

Feeling defeated, I blow the list off and watch Ultimate Fighting on cable for an hour, work out in the gym, then spend the remainder of the morning in the lobby, glued to my laptop, looking for titles to the Fox Island properties, Michigan-based charitable foundations of the seventies, Adam Starchild, and two committee members in the Fox Island Lighthouse Association alongside John McKinney Jr., even though I still cannot prove that Fox Island is directly linked to the case.

In 1978, shortly after the OCCK murders ended, I find, the Department of Natural Resources' Waterways Division set a new list of ecological goals for South Fox Island, one of which was to preserve the integrity of, and protect from desecration, an ancient gravesite on the land. Somewhere in my stack of papers there's an official statement from a cleared suspect in the OCCK murders in which he directs the police to "go up there north" if they wanted to find the truth. Shelden's island, North Fox, was scoured at the time, with the police reportedly turning up nothing of substance. South Fox was apparently never touched, but was later discovered to have been used for drug-running operations.

• • •

I get Chinese takeout for lunch, eat it in my room, and watch more Ultimate Fighting. I try to nap. I get up and shower during a rainstorm that's set in. When the water is spraying my face, I think I hear a window sliding open.

I get out and pull back the curtains, stand in my towel after I've showered. The window hasn't been moved, I don't think. I watch the rain until it clears and becomes a red swath in the distance over Northwestern Highway.

I keep thinking about Fox Island being another skeleton key, like the prosecutor's offices, that will open every door.

TERMINAL

On July Fourth, my wedding anniversary, I call my kids early, knowing they'll be out watching fireworks tonight. I don't reach them, leaving a voice message instead. I spend the early part of the night in my hotel room watching cable, eating barbecued ribs and collard greens from a local soul food carryout, and listening to bottle rockets go off outside the hotel.

I feel lonely. The Fourth is normally a family night for us. We don't celebrate our anniversary but we always went to the fireworks, which I never really enjoyed but tolerated yearly to witness the joy my kids found in them. I thought of this as creating memories, but what my kids will likely remember is not my admiration of their folly but the grimace I sometimes wore with each explosion. When I think of fireworks, I think of fingers being blown off, or of being at summer camp one year when a boy taped a cherry bomb to the belly of a frog, or the images of Holocaust victims I was forced to watch in Hebrew school on a black-and-white reel-to-reel, how the bodies were lined up and stacked like already-charred wood, how the dead had been burned into their dying.

It's macabre, I know.

I watch cable until midnight, mostly more news about Tot Mom. Reporter Nancy Grace won't shut up about it. Ms. Anthony certainly looks guilty, but a trial, if the system is working, will determine that in the end.

The OCCK grand jury, I soon learn from Cathy, will disband without charges being brought and without anybody in the public knowing what or whom was discussed. In the absence of a working system, like in the OCCK case, there is only private investigation and public appeal. Sometimes people appear to contemplate violence. Like Tom Ascroft once told me, "The prosecutor's worst nightmare is that I get diagnosed with a terminal illness, because then what's going to stop me?"

In his position, I might consider violence, too. An eye for an eye, when you're out of options, can seem reasonable. I hope I'm not another overzealous reporter, a one-man lynch mob in my assumptions about the case. This is why I haven't returned any calls from members of the press, several of whom have gotten a line on my cell.

I want to be sure about what I know and don't know before I talk to anybody.

• • •

IN THE MORNING I start making calls, trying to track what happened to Reni Lelek, the female police officer from the newspaper photograph beside Tim King and John McKinney, Birmingham's first female officer. I call newspapers, I call police stations. When I find out Reni's actually alive, I just sit there on the edge of my bed with my cell phone in my hand. *The ghost is walking,* I think. *How could I have been so wrong? What made me think she was dead?* The Birmingham PD tells me that Reni retired a few years ago and lives in Arizona. I try to find her on Facebook but can't. I find someone who appears to be her daughter, though, still living in Michigan.

I dig a little deeper and get a work number for the woman, but when I call they won't put me through. Everybody has moved on. Maybe I should, too, I think. It's eleven a.m. and I haven't eaten breakfast. I'll go do that, I think, but when I get into my car, I end up skipping food and merging onto the freeway back to Dexter, where I park again and walk into the nature preserve.

The air is wet and the smell of foliage fills my lungs and I sit on a large outcropping and stare off and think about Reni.

My sister, whom I'd been unable to get ahold of, calls me on my cell and I answer quickly. She sounds frantic. Her husband is coming home from a vacation with his parents, and she needs to get her house cleaned, she says. Then she doesn't say anything for a while, and I just listen to the silence with her.

"I don't want you to leave, Jason," she says finally.

"I know," I say.

"I feel sad. You're always welcome at my house," she tells me.

"I know it," I say. "I wish I lived here, but I don't." When I say it, I know it's true, this wanting to be near to her, to Detroit, to something like pain, but the kind of pain that feels like home to me.

When we hang up, I lie back on the outcropping, thinking of my sister and of how to get in touch with Reni. My skin is damp from the humidity and a slight breeze eventually chills me for a minute. *I don't feel very fucking good,* I want to tell somebody, but there's nobody to tell it to. Maybe I'm grasping at straws. Maybe I didn't come out here to prove I can solve the case, but to prove that I cannot.

HAPPY BIRTHDAY, TIM

I have dinner with Teresa at a Thai placc in Birmingham. I stare at her throughout dinner, and she's silent after claiming she's tired. I find myself wondering if I could spend my life with her.

We sit in the park near the Birmingham Police Department and eat ice cream after dinner. I stare at the small brick building where the Birmingham PD lost their part of this case to the Michigan State Police in the 1970s. Nothing about the building has changed, only right now the flowers around it are in bloom with a series of sprinklers popping up in small bursts instead of the deadly cold air that surrounded it during the winters of '76 and '77.

Teresa and I take a walk through a neighborhood of Mayberry-like homes where a teenaged boy on a longboard dive-bombs a hill out front of his house. We watch him and then Teresa hugs me and we stand in the street like that. I can hear the kid laughing at the end of his block, where a girl hugs him and mimics us.

Back in my hotel, alone, I get a text from Teresa.

My favorite part was the walk, she says.

Me too, I text her back.

I'd wanted those kids' lives down at the bottom of the hill, mimicking what it'd meant to be old and on your way out.

At three a.m. I wake from a dream in which Cathy's oldest still-living brother, Chris, won't speak to me because I've drawn attention to the case and put their father under a microscope by the press and police.

In real life, the cops called Barry King this week and requested his DNA, but it wasn't the Michigan State Police or the Oakland County Prosecutor's Office who called, it was a Detective Don Studt, an original task force member whom the Internet sleuth Helen Dagner appeared to have a convivial relationship with, as witnessed by dozens of email and snail mail correspondences between the two, spanning years. Detective Studt telephoned King at his residence and requested a cheek swab.

I sleep briefly again, then wake before dawn wondering why Erica McAvoy, Kristine's sister, hasn't returned a few phone calls I'd recently placed to her. She hasn't returned my emails, either. Maybe she's intuiting that I want to ask her about the document containing possibly revealing information from back in 1977 about her mom's boyfriend, a guy who used to visit her mom while she was bartending at Hartfield

Lanes. The document says this guy, her mom's lover, was an associate of John at the time, the man who Helen Dagner maintains confessed to her in the Big Boy in Alpena, but it doesn't say how they were known to one another.

When questioned about the boyfriend years later, Erica and Kristine's mom denied the man's existence. Maybe she was protecting somebody, even herself, or maybe she truly never knew a man who knew John. In either case, she refused public statements for thirty years, and I'm suspicious of that—not of the implications of silence, but of the strength of conviction needed to silence oneself.

Today, I realize, is Timothy King's birthday.

FATHERS

I've driven back to Barry King's house to retrieve the extra files that he's set aside for me, about two thousand pages of transcripts from the state police and FBI, some of which even Barry hasn't read yet.

I park in the street and walk up to the front door, where I notice the doorknob has become worn with age. It's the same doorknob Timmy, as Barry calls him sometimes, would have twisted to come in and out of the house. I look around at the tidy yard. A lot of money has been spent on landscaping, but the doorknob is exactly as it should be: familiar, just in case.

I sit in the living room with Barry King and his relatively new wife, whom he calls his "bride." Tim's mom has long passed by now, and Barry's nearing eighty but he still has a youthful smile widening between rosy cheeks. Reading glasses hang around his neck, and he appears to be extremely sharp, vibrant almost, although he's walking slower and says he's feeling more tired than he did at seventy-five. We chat, and then Barry's wife busies herself in the kitchen while

I'm shown the documents. I take them in my car to a FedEx Office and spend two and a half hours photocopying them, looking over my shoulder.

When I get back to Barry's house, I peek into the downstairs office at an old photo of Tim in his hockey uniform. It's been a popular photo in the press all these years, so I feel almost like I'm looking at an original Babe Ruth baseball card, at history. When I'm back in my car later, I think about how much Barry loved his son, how much any man loves his son and would go crazy in Barry's position.

I'M ON THE freeway and I get a call from my dad. My kids are coming to visit me in a few days, and he's scheduled to take us to a Tigers game. We've all been looking forward to it, especially my son. But when my dad calls, he's upset at me for other time constraints I've placed on him. The kids will be here only for a week, and I want them to see old friends, not just my dad. I've told him that we can visit during the ball game and then maybe go to dinner another night. But my dad wants more than that, and he gets angry when he can't have it.

I explain our schedule. I tell my dad that I'm taking the kids to Lake Michigan.

I say, "We're spread thin." I want my kids to visit with my sister, and I want them to meet my dad's son from his second marriage, Max, who will be visiting from Florida, where he's attending college.

My dad hasn't spoken to Max in at least five years. It's no different with Max than it was with me as a kid, growing up trying to figure out how much love is the right amount of love to let yourself give to this man, and, afterward, to anybody else. My dad, when he hears that I'm going to see Max, launches into a tirade.

"You're going to shunt me aside?" he says. I can hear his pulse rising through the shakiness of his breath. I don't answer him. I feel so many things, some of them fear. "You want to keep your fucking kids from me?"

I try to keep my eyes on the road but my pulse has risen to meet my father's. I feel the road swerving in front of me on the freeway.

"Hey," he says after a few beats. "Fuck you and fuck your kids. They don't ever have to know who their grandfather is."

I feel like I'm seven again. I'm about to get hurt or I'm just in trouble and I don't know why and even though I sense that I've done nothing to deserve whatever happens, I still feel guilty for my father's anger.

I pull onto the shoulder of the freeway, spraying up gravel behind me until my car stops. I can hear my father hollering at me through the phone but I place it on the dash now, on speaker, and I press my face to the steering wheel while I breathe.

I feel like I'm supposed to make things better.

"You want to go to the ball game?" he continues, shouting. "Then go to the fucking ball game. I'll put the tickets in my mailbox!" I can hear him breathing heavily, and then he finally says, "What do you think about that?"

I wait a long time and then I take him off speaker and I tell him, quietly, "You've never come to visit your grandkids. My son is twelve and he doesn't know who you are. My daughter saw you once, when she was six. That was ten years ago."

"So what?" he says.

Cars are flying by me on the freeway.

After a while of not answering him, I just hang up.

I check a voice message that came through while my father was yelling. It's Erica, finally returning my messages. She wants me to drive to Okemos tonight and have dinner with her and her father.

It's late afternoon already and I'm riding the cut between two worlds, my own father on one side, the victims' fathers on the other. I do an illegal U-turn across the median and take the freeway back north.

ERICA AND HER father, Tom, and I meet at the Stillwater Grill again. During our three-hour dinner, Erica tells me that she's researched some of the Busch family holdings of the era and has discovered that Christopher Busch, just days before the "suicide" (she air quotes), had quitclaimed his ownership of the restaurant he worked in, signing it over to his dad, who was in Europe at the time. The timing is suspicious.

Erica is eating pasta. I think Tom is recording our conversation with his cell phone. When I ask Erica about her mom and the alleged boyfriend who claimed to know John, I get the feeling she's pretending not to remember anything. I don't feel like fucking around anymore.

BITS OF HAIR

A grand jury's purpose is to decide whether or not the prosecution has gathered enough evidence to bring the case against a person or entity to trial; it's not the trial itself. While a grand jury in this case—alas, after over three decades of waiting—is exciting, it doesn't mean that things will end well for the families. In fact, it could be the opposite, as Cathy predicts.

If the prosecutor wants to clear Christopher Busch and Gregory Greene and put an end to any speculation by the public or, in this case, by the families of the victims, the easiest way to do that might be to call a grand jury and present a flimsy case for prosecution. The grand jury would reject the case, and the prosecutor would be off the hook for the Busch and Greene leads. The prosecutor would now be able to deflect in other directions indefinitely; no more looking into Busch and Greene.

Calling for a grand jury may also be an attempt by the prosecutor to freeze out the press for a while. By federal law, no police personnel or other involved party is allowed to speak about

244

information being secretly deliberated upon in a grand jury. A grand jury buys the prosecutor time, but for what?

The arrows pointing toward Busch and Greene are accumulating in my head, but these guys were unhinged individuals with multiple charges prior to the OCCK murders and were not off-the-grid types. They were slobs with voracious appetites for self-destruction. They certainly were not the obsessive-compulsive, meticulous, sophisticated killers the police had reportedly been pretending to hunt after for three and a half decades. Busch and Greene, I have to believe, lead to something bigger and more worthy of protection than just H. Lee Busch's reputation.

Just as Mark Stebbins was found with animal hairs and other fibers on him, all three of the other known OCCK victims were also found with animal hair fragments, in addition to the human hair fragments on both Kristine Mihelich and Jill Robinson. The small white animal hairs on all exterior clothing are assumed to have come from a canine, likely a terrier. In addition, gold- or yellow-colored fibers were found on both of the boys but not on the girls. What we can reasonably assume is that the white dog hairs were from the interior of a vehicle used to transport each of the children at some point during their captivity, but that the boys and girls were actually housed separately, the boys at a location with gold-

or yellow-colored carpeting and the girls at a location that left no fibers on them, like a wood-floored home or a concrete garage.

If this is true, we can likely say that the abductors were not necessarily the killers, and we can also speculate that Greene and Busch could very well have been involved in housing only the boys. Indeed, the evidence related to Busch and Greene points strongly to involvement with Stebbins's and King's murders only.

Who, then, was responsible for Robinson and Mihelich during their captivity, and what was done to them? No evidence of sexual penetration was found on the two girls, not semen nor blood evidence, it was routinely stated by police, although a March 17, 1977, newspaper article reported that "an autopsy found evidence of sexual assault, while a crime lab investigator found none." Regardless of this discrepancy, based on the DNA match to Vincent Gunnels's hair on Kristine, and his explanation, it can be reasonably assumed that Kristine at least traveled in Busch's vehicle at some point during her abduction.

Based on that, it is easy to conclude that Christopher Busch was, at the very least, a delivery boy for a client whose taste was female, while Busch and Greene kept the boys for either themselves or another client. The white animal hairs would have come from either the automobile or the clothing of Christopher Busch, whose family pet was a small white terrier.

In 1995 the Wayne County Detectives Bureau collected hair fibers from the sauna room at a facility whose name is redacted from the documents. Fibers were collected from beneath the surfaces of benches and from the sill beneath the sauna doorway. The Schvitz sits squarely in my field of speculation. Detective Garry Gray pulled that evidence fourteen years later, in 2009, but the documents don't show where that evidence might be today.

I know, however, that none of the evidence ever catalogued can now be compared to Christopher Busch, since his father cremated the body instead of opting for the more traditional burial method of the time. Who, then, was Detective Gray analyzing the sauna hairs against, and what happened in 1995 to push Wayne County in that direction?

Right before I fall asleep amid the documents, I get a text from Cathy, reminding me of a suspect I haven't yet paid much attention to:

Check on Norberg, she texts me.

Then she adds, **Check on Ray Anger. That fucker is dirty, Jason.**

TIGERS

I receive an email from my dad, apologizing for what he calls his "apoplectic" behavior. I have to look up the word to realize he's only apologizing for being the same jerk he always was. My kids are arriving in two days. If I can help it, he's not wrapping them into a cycle of abuse. He's afraid of getting close, afraid of intimacy, and so he bails, but I can make a choice to protect them from that.

A ball game is still in the works, but I can't afford decent tickets. On my budget, we'll be sitting in the nosebleeds. I bite the bullet and drive to my dad's neighborhood, flip the car around, and pull up to his mailbox. I pull an unmarked envelope from it, then close the mailbox again. When I'm leaving his subdivision I open the envelope, and inside it are the three crisp season tickets he'd been hollering about, with seats down the first-base line. My dad's held back his own ticket, no doubt intending to show up and surprise us after I've already told the kids some unlikely scenario about why their grandfather won't be at the game. I resent him most of all for this, for making me, after all these years, still somehow subject to his whims.

In a moment of grace, I realize that I can tell my kids what is both true and a lie at the same time. I can say: *Grandpa is sick. He might come to the game, and he might not.*

I PICKED MY kids up from the airport, held them in my arms near the gate for as long as they'd let me. My son, twelve, arrived with a faux hawk haircut I'd never seen on him. He'd grown in my absence. My daughter, sixteen, was like a reed, sinewy and strong, hovering protectively beside her little brother in the crowded airport terminal as we walked.

During that week with them, we met up with my old friends, visited old restaurants, and saw my old homes, including the one in Ann Arbor where my wife and I had lived with our daughter over a decade ago, before our son was born.

We visited with my dad's ex, Paula, and their son together, my half brother Max, now in his twenties, and they took us on a boat ride on the lake behind Paula's house in Bloomfield. My son did backflips into the water off the boat. At full throttle, I watched my daughter's hair push back in the wind, studied the depths of her eyes. I could tell that she wanted to be a part of a universe that would allow her continued movement like that, at greater and greater speeds, toward something larger-than-life. With the sunlight on my boy's face and the wind in his wet hair, I felt powerful. He'd miraculously inherited the parts of me that had gone unscathed, and I would defend those parts of him forever.

We went on a lengthy side trip to Lake Michigan, where we spent two days in the artsy beach town of Saugatuck visiting with my aunt and uncle, who'd timed their own vacation from Delaware to coincide with our arrival. As a boy, my mom had shipped me out to them a few times, during summer and winter breaks, as a respite from the chaos of my family. I sometimes looked back at those weeks I'd spent in Delaware as the healthiest weeks of my childhood.

My aunt and uncle took us to dinner and ice cream. We strolled the boardwalk by the lake afterward, the sun sinking into twilight. I felt whole suddenly. I felt that I was living the life I'd been meant to live, my children by my side and the breeze off Lake Michigan vibrant, the notion of happiness somehow greater than a notion again.

WE GO TO the Tigers game at the end of that week. I'm nervous in the strong afternoon heat. We push through a crowd, looking for our seats, where we find my father waiting for us. I shake my father's hand. I tell him that we're leaving after the fifth inning so my daughter can take pictures of the city. It's a lie I've made up on the spot. He says nothing to me in return.

My father shakes my son's hand and says, looking him over, "I think I'm getting you a hairbrush for your birthday." It's the first time they've met, the first thing he's said to the boy, ever.

Then he kisses my daughter on the cheek and says back to my son, "I don't kiss boys. Sorry."

My father laughs loudly at the joke. My son flushes. I can smell aftershave and alcohol on my dad.

When we take our seats, I position myself between my dad and the kids. The players are called onto the field, and when we stand for the National Anthem, my dad holds his beer to his chest and belts out the words like an opera singer.

People in front of us turn to look.

Nobody else in our section is singing.

My dad drinks two more large beers during the game. He buys the kids some ice cream and ball caps. After the fifth inning, he walks us to an exit, spilling one of his beers and cursing. "Fuck they put that floor there for?" he says.

I don't often swear around my kids. When my dad does it, they look at me to see my reaction. I hold their look, smiling.

At the exit, my dad shakes my hand good-bye. He shakes my son's hand, very formally. Then he hugs my daughter, and when he pulls back from the hug, his fingers linger on her shoulder, his palm cupping her arm like a baseball mitt, and I don't like him touching her, because in my world you have to earn getting to touch somebody affectionately.

Isn't that what he taught me? And isn't that what I'd never earned from him, all the times I'd tried to hug him as a boy and he'd stiff-arm me with a handshake?

HELLO, GOOD-BYE

My kids get on a plane back to Idaho, and I stay in my hotel for two days, watching the television and sleeping atop a pile of notes on my bed. I'm dark inside again.

On the third day Teresa calls to drag me out of my room. I agree to her visiting with lunch. I get out of bed and work in the hotel lobby, waiting for her. There are now two grand juries convened, I've learned, in both Wayne and Oakland Counties. Barry King has been served a subpoena to testify, but he only hints at that on the telephone. If I press him for details, I risk setting him up for a felony charge, Cathy has warned me—something about the rules of grand jury secrecy overriding our usual expectation of public trial—so I don't.

I feel a little better when Teresa enters the hotel lobby with another large grocery bag of food for us.

Sitting in the lobby with Teresa is nice. The sun comes through a large window and lights her skin. I can see marks on her face from age, strands of greying hair grasping for larger purchase. Maybe it's okay that she's here. She has no children that she's compromising, no marriage vows. Maybe the two of us are working on love again, soberly but not sadly. Just clear-minded, human love that comes out of patience and caring.

I walk Teresa to her car after a two-hour lunch and I kiss her. It takes time. It's 100 degrees outside with the sun banking into us from the asphalt, and I know, deeply, that my guilt over Teresa's relationship, and over my own, will have a larger hold on me now. That single kiss is a hello and a good-bye at the same time.

We embrace one another, and when I'm walking back to the hotel without her I can feel the sweat holding my shirt down across the midsection of my back where her arms had crossed. I don't have much time left in Detroit, and there's so much to do. I want to know whose hand closed the mouths of those kids, and I wonder if spending time with Teresa is a way of putting off the realization that I may not get what I want with this case.

LAMBORGINE

Ted Lamborgine, dimed on by Richard Lawson as being connected to the OCCK killings, is seventy-five years old and serving three life sentences for unrelated crimes in a Michigan prison, which is not to say that he had no connection to Christopher Busch and Gregory Greene.

Lamborgine is bald, with the exception of tufts of grey swooping around the sides of his head. In photos, he either wears squared-off wire-framed glasses or no glasses at all, revealing a paling canvas of a face, hued primarily by prison lighting, no doubt. As a convicted pedophile, he likely spent the early years of his incarceration, at the age of sixty-five, being assaulted by other convicts, unable to protect himself at such an advanced age for that environment.

Prior to his capture, Lamborgine was living a relatively mundane life three hours southeast of Detroit, in Parma Heights, Ohio. He was a retired autoworker, lying low beneath the radar of the police until pedophile turned confidential informant Richard Lawson's arrest for that 1989 cabbie murder. Lawson's testimony during his murder trial shed new light on the 1970s Cass Corridor pedophile ring. Lawson pointed at Ted Lamborgine's involvement with the Cass operation and fingered him as an OCCK suspect.

In 2005, PD traveled to Parma Heights and took Lamborgine into custody for his involvement with the Cass crimes. In 2007, Lamborgine confessed to using money, drugs, and food as a lure for dozens of young boys who were abducted into hotel rooms, homes, and a bicycle shop, where they were sexually assaulted in order to make pornographic movies sold throughout the U.S. and Europe via an East Coast hub.

Prior to Lamborgine's sentencing, he was given an OCCK-related polygraph, which he failed. He was offered a plea deal that would allow him safe haven in a more cozy federal prison, under witness protection, at a reduced sentence of fifteen years if he would confess to his involvement in the killings. Lamborgine turned down the deal, which might make one believe he had nothing to offer and therefore no deal to broker. Yet, during his initial interrogation, with the police breathing down his neck about the OCCK murders, Lamborgine's only response had been "I've been forgiven."

Knowing that he was unable to be charged with the OCCK crimes without a confession, due to lack of hard evidence, Lamborgine accepted a sentence that secured the promise of dying while still in custody instead of the fifteen years he could have gotten in a plea to the OCCK crimes. He either had no knowledge of the murders or was afraid of detailing his involvement.

When speaking to the press on multiple occasions, Detectives Garry Gray and Ray Anger had opposing theories about Lamborgine. Gray was adamant about Ted Lamborgine's association with the OCCK, but Ray Anger was quoted as saying, "[Lamborgine] said he didn't do it, and I don't think he did." Anger had seemingly little to do with the investigation of Lamborgine, however, while Gray was involved with the initial interrogations alongside the younger cop, Cory Williams, the star detective from that *Cold Case* episode about Richard Lawson I'd watched in my hotel room a while back.

If Anger is dirty, as Cathy had texted me before the Tigers game, then there must be motivation for publicly pronouncing his belief in Lamborgine's innocence related to the OCCK. If you follow Lamborgine, where does he lead?

After reading through thousands of pages of interview transcription, one thing I am certain of is that Detective Anger seems to be of relatively common intelligence, while Cory Williams possesses a more honed intellect. His interviews with suspects read like some of our classical stage dramas, within which the true weight of a statement or question remains unknown to all but its speaker until the second or third act, when what was presumably a throwaway line comes back to haunt the play. Anger, in transcription, attempts to lasso an answer, whereas Williams opens a door, steps back, and allows each answer to cross the threshold into a snare of its own accord.

Cory Williams, of the Livonia Police Department and a generation younger than Anger, was so convinced of Lamborgine's involvement with the OCCK crimes that he doggedly pursued the connection for years. He made eight trips to Parma Heights, with six separate surveillance operations performed in Ohio by the Michigan State Police, the FBI, and Livonia PD, as well as conducted numerous out-of-state interviews with Lamborgine's past victims who had relocated to Tennessee, Mississippi, Florida, Arizona, and the Netherlands.

Of interest relating to the opposing viewpoints of Cory Williams and Ray Anger is that, while Anger was a Berkley, Michigan, cop during the 1970s, so, too, was Williams's own father, serving as a lieutenant with the Berkley PD at the same time. One has to consider, then, a legacy of information about the OCCK that might have been passed down from Williams Sr., long out of the force by now, and subsequently inquire: Is Cory Williams operating with a private, personal mandate to clean house on behalf of his old man?

If the answer is yes, then Cory Williams might be the only cop I can trust. Unfortunately, since the Wayne County grand jury has also been called, Williams isn't answering his telephone when I try him, nor is he responding to my messages. Even operating in the dark, however, some people believe that Cory Williams won't stop until a few of his father's contemporaries wind up on the wrong side of the headlines.

Lamborgine, for his part, living out hard time beneath prison halogens, remains silent.

PEABODY'S

I go to the Berkley library near the Roseland Park Cemetery because of a reference in the documents given to me by Barry King about a 1976 junior class Berkley High photograph of a boy, another victim of Christopher Busch. The librarian glances at the self-imposed bruise on my cheek, then leads me to a small shelving unit.

I sit at a wooden table and look through yearbooks from '75 to '78. One of the boys stands out, smiling at the camera, head cocked slightly, his brown hair sweeping sideways across his forehead like a young Justin Bieber. I remember reading his name in interviews, yet the details are foggy. I'm starting to lose my memory of things previously read.

I've missed something, I think.

I put my head on the table and wrap my arms around its crown, and when I sit up again an hour has passed and I've drooled on the '76 volume.

ON THE WAY out of Berkley, I drive by Hartfield Lanes and park out front of the covered entrance to the bowling alley. Kristine Mihelich was most likely taken from this entranceway, or from across the street at the 7-Eleven, in January 1977.

I stay parked outside of Hartfield's. I touch the small bruise on my cheekbone. I look at it in the rearview mirror and touch it again but don't feel anything.

I call Timothy's brother, Chris King, on my cell, and he talks to me about two cops from the original investigative team, a cop named Flynn and a cop named Waldron, who died last January. Cory Williams supposedly talked to Waldron at some point prior to his death, and Waldron cried when Williams told him that the Busch polygraph results were wrong.

Waldron wanted the case solved. The tears seemed real to Williams, Chris reports, and I can hear him breathing heavily into the phone. I met Chris on my first trip to Detroit and we sat at his kitchen table going over link charts of the case. Chris was thick-bodied and seemed tough but had a copy editor's intellect and eye for detail. A lot of native Detroiters are like that, even in some of the nearby suburbs: able to pass for the muscle or the brains, depending on the moment. When your daily living is a grind, you get dull or you get sharp, and Chris seemed the latter.

Over the phone, Chris reminds me about the blue Gremlin at the pharmacy on the night of his brother's abduction—how he, like the witness who came forward, also saw the vehicle, only much later at night than the reported time of abduction. The cops were already out searching for Tim when Chris, a teenager at that time, searching on his own, saw a Gremlin and a few other empty cars in the pharmacy parking lot several hours after Tim's disappearance.

By morning the blue Gremlin was gone. The alleged witness, who provided information for a composite sketch of the Gremlin, came forward only after the long initial night of Tim's captivity. Chris maintains that he told the police back then that his brother must have been kidnapped into another vehicle. Tim couldn't have been in the blue Gremlin, he told them, as that car hadn't left the lot until hours had passed. The Gremlin, Chris believed then as now, was a red herring.

It's possible that two vehicles were involved in the abduction of Timothy King, both men jumping into one car with the boy, leaving the Gremlin behind overnight. If true, that may have been an on-the-fly error, which does sometimes happen even in well-planned crimes. Home-land terrorist Timothy McVeigh was taken into custody in 1995 only after being pulled over for driving a car with no license plate on it. Three days later he was identified as the mastermind behind the bombing of the Alfred P. Murrah Federal Building in Oklahoma City. He had calculated a highly detailed mass murder, one of the most complicated acts of terrorism our country has seen, but was grounded by the sometimes more complicated twists of fate that often look like blind stupidity in retrospect.

I get off the phone with Chris and stop back at Barry King's to get another thousand documents he's set aside for me to copy. On my way back from the FedEx Office, I pass the restaurant where Barry and his wife were eating dinner on the night of Tim's abduction: Peabody's, in Birmingham, just down the street from their home.

The restaurant is catty-corner from the pharmacy at Maple Road. It's possible that Barry and his wife glanced up from their meals at the traffic outside on that March night, the streaming headlights absorbed into slush or glinting off street signs and flecks of snow in the air, with Timmy in the back of one of those passing cars.

THESE FUCKING COPS

I talk to Barry at length when I return to his house. Twenty years ago, he says, the convict Richard Lawson called him from prison saying he knew something about the OCCK murders. He wanted to have a conversation. He asked Barry King to come visit him.

Barry didn't visit Lawson but he told the police about the call. Detective Don Studt from the original task force, the cop who'd had that long-running correspondence with the Internet sleuth Helen Dagner, interviewed Lawson and said Lawson had reiterated his testimony that Lamborgine had a connection to the case. Barry said there wasn't any reason to trust Lawson at the time because it seemed like he wanted to leverage that information for personal gain. Convicts lie, he said. The cops wouldn't look into it.

In 2012, Richard Lawson reached out again and wrote Barry King a letter. Dave Binkley, Barry's attorney, drove out to talk with Lawson. Lawson told Binkley that he and a man named Bobby Moore used to "get boys" for H. Lee Busch, Christopher Busch's father.

Barry also tells me some minor details of interest: that Detroit reporter Kevin Dietz, known for doing stories on the OCCK, also went to Brother Rice High School, whose alumni include John, the suspect who Helen Dagner maintains confessed to her, as well as the famous *Dateline NBC* reporter Chris Hansen. The King family recently called Hansen in the hopes that he would do a story on the case, but they got the brush-off from his producers.

Barry's conjecture about the two grand juries is that Wayne County may be examining what's become known in small circles as "the Wasser polygraph" as it relates to the Busch lead—the King family is adamant that Busch implicated himself in the killings during that private polygraph administered by Larry Wasser—while Oakland County may be following up on the Cass and Fox leads. An insider from the grand jury team has recently called Barry King, I learn from Cathy, who won't tell me her source but insists that it's not her father, and revealed that a forensic detective has turned over three human hairs from Mark Stebbins.

Later, Barry discloses to me that, in November of 2009, a man named Tim Nummer, who used to play hockey with Tim as a boy, came to Barry's house and told him that seventeen years earlier, in 1992, he sold some clothing to a few cops in a retail store he worked at. While ringing them up, he casually asked the cops about the Timothy King case. One of the cops said, "Oh, that's been solved. He was killed by the son of some auto exec who was turned in by his attorney."

Tim Nummer, Barry says, came by again just two weeks before my own visit. He told Barry he would go public about his interaction with those cops if it would help. Barry shared this offer with a Detroit news reporter named Heather Catallo, investigator Cory Williams, the Michigan State Police, and Rob Moran of the Wayne County Prosecutor's Office. Not one of those people followed up. Tim Nummer's statements to Barry were circumstantial, they rightly said.

Barry also told me that he thinks Gregory Greene was in jail at the time of Tim's murder. Everybody outside of the police thinks that, although a note on an internal narrative summary from the initial investigation specifically states that Greene was out on bond at the time of Tim's abduction and killing.

THAT NIGHT AT dusk I go to a coffee shop near the Lodge Freeway, get a black coffee, and sit outside on a curb watching the traffic streaming toward downtown. I call Chris King again and he tells me that, in approximately 2005, Detective Don Studt told him that there was no evidence in the case whatsoever—not even close. He told Chris, "Look, you have to come to terms

266

with the fact that this case will never be solved."

The only possibility, he said to Chris, was a deathbed confession. "And even then," Studt said, "I wouldn't believe it unless there were Polaroids."

"Who do we fucking kill to get a confession, then?" I joke with Chris.

Chris says, "Believe me . . ." and then he trails off.

He eventually remarks on how Christopher Busch ended up dead soon after his polygraph. Then he pauses again and says finally, "I don't know if they're just doing a vigilante job or they're cleaning up their own mess from back then."

He says you can't get a confession if everybody dies quick, and his frustration is palpable and expected, regardless of whether or not either of us knows the truth at this point.

The cell phone is hot against my ear before I hang up.

At least Richard Lawson, the convict who dimed on Lamborgine, is still alive and, as far as I know at the time, serving a life sentence for the cabdriver murder that Cory Williams tagged him on. Maybe he'll talk to me but probably not, I think.

Chris King also tells me that a woman from the area, now a friend of Cathy's, had reached out to John's brother online.

"The brother had said to Cathy's friend, 'Oh, yeah, John knew Chris Busch, absolutely!'" Then Chris breathes into the phone and says, "But we got all these cops who say there's no connection?"

I speculate that it might be Helen Dagner ruining the John lead for everybody, a kill-the-messenger scenario. The cops are not well-disposed toward obsessive amateurs. Chris sort of grunts into his end of the line. "I wouldn't doubt it," he says.

He reiterates the death dates of some key players for me. I write it all down again because it's hard to keep track:

- McKinney was killed in September of 1977.
- The cop named Flynn was a suicide on November 14, 1978.
- Christopher Busch was found on November 20, 1978, but it appeared he might have been bloating a few days before he was found, putting his death date even closer to Flynn's.
- Bobby Moore, who was Lamborgine's roommate, was found dead in 1978 or '79, Chris tries to remember, eaten by his own pit bulls in the drug house he lived in. It was either a murder or a suicide, but nobody could tell after the dogs had chewed him up.

"But if it was cops cleaning up dirty laundry," Chris says, "they must have realized they'd only scratched the surface."

That's when they took out McKinney in September of '77, according to Chris's theory.

The cops went into McKinney's gallery, he speculates, and they beat him up a little to get more information before shooting him. They also stole the rope sculpture that was never found and was among the least expensive items to steal. If the McKinney murder had been a robbery and not an assassination, items of greater value would have been taken, Chris reminds me.

Soon after McKinney's murder, Chris Busch is dead, he says.

Then Chris King tells me about the "Berkley Witness," a guy who'd been posting online under a pseudonym. I am aware of the identity of the Berkley Witness but am using a pseudonym here and calling him Sebastian. While Sebastian's story is believable to me and to at least some others, I cannot ignore that he may have descended or at least dipped into one of the rabbit holes that pocket my own inquiries. It may be that his tale can be further substantiated or denied, but I am leaving that for others. For this reason, too, I am not naming the police officers who he discusses beyond saying that they are names familiar to the OCCK case files.

At some point, Sebastian and Cathy had connected, Chris relays to me. Sebastian told Cathy
that he'd seen Kristine talking to a cop at the
7-Eleven on the day of her abduction.

Sebastian was in third grade at the time, and
after Kristine had turned up dead, he told his
mother about seeing her a few days earlier. After
they went to the Berkley cops about it, Sebastian
says, his life became a living hell.

Sebastian, at least, is somebody alive.

SWAG

I t's late. I'm in the Cass, driving the darkened streets. Two guys are on the porch of a squatter's home staring at me as I roll past. The last thing Chris King told me on the phone was that Jack Kalbfleisch, the original task force member I'd had a call with while I was at the mall, had recently sent a letter to multiple police departments complaining that a rear bumper imprint of a Pontiac LeMans from the snow at the Kristine site wasn't being taken seriously.

"It turns out, Ray Anger is the contact for the bumper imprint," Chris had said. I remember Cathy's late-night text to me: *That fucker is dirty.*

It was Anger, too, who'd dug up the body of a suspect named Norberg in Montana, having booked a flight on his own dime to do it. Norberg had been under suspicion in the early days but wasn't focused on, the cops having Busch on their radar and Norberg's wife having provided multiple alibis for him.

In 2006, the OCCK victims' families had a meeting with the PD and Anger was there, along with Garry Gray. They both pleaded for

271

the families to "keep things out of the media" but that begged the question: Which things, and why? After three decades, surely the investigation would no longer be compromised by *more* information provided to the public rather than *less*. And yet Gray was a short-timer to retirement, while Anger maybe had something else to protect, according to the speculation of several people I've talked to in addition to Chris King.

Chris King's theory on why Anger visited Norberg's grave is contrary to the official release statements. In the press, the exhumation was reportedly due to a necklace found at Norberg's home prior to his death, an insignia charm that read "Kristine," but Kristine's parents don't remember her having a charm like that. Chris King's theory is that Anger concocted the necklace excuse to dig up Norberg and test his DNA against a hair found on Tim for some other, self-serving reason.

What Anger didn't do, I learn from internal case narratives, was compare DNA to any of the other evidence catalogued in the case files. He only compared Norberg's DNA to the single trace hair on Tim. According to Chris King, Anger probably already knew the hair wouldn't match Norberg's DNA. In testing him publicly, Anger was taking a shortcut to ruling out Norberg and dropping all further speculation with his reburial, King theorized.

IN THE LATE 1980s, Ray Anger took Erica McAvoy to get hypnotized, presumably to see if she could remember anything about the necklace he said was found in Norberg's residence during the initial police inquiries into him. The whole afternoon, Erica told Chris, she felt like Anger was a creep. He wanted to go to lunch after the hypnosis session and took her to a McDonald's, where she felt he became too personal in his affectations, too camp with her.

In 2010, Erica called Ray Anger and told him she had some questions about the case. He was charismatic in tone. He said, when questioned, "Chris Busch has been excluded due to lack of DNA evidence."

It was a misdirect, as Chris Busch had *not* officially been excluded. To the contrary, Busch was still very much on the books as a suspect in 2010. Anger ended their conversation with "Honey, you're welcome to call me anytime." It was a throwback to the phoniness she sensed from years past.

I GET OUT of my car at the Brewster Projects and sit on the hood. There's a breeze like a death rattle coming from the hollowed-out tenements.

Up ahead of me, two young black guys in swagger jeans and curtain-sized white Ts approach at a snail's pace in the middle of the street. There's no light across their bodies except from a single bulb a dozen houses down. I watch them getting closer for a long time, eventually smell the menthol from their cigarettes in the dark. The drift of nicotine turns my chest inward, sets me on edge.

When the two guys pass, they stare at me. One of them flicks his cigarette at my car. I don't turn my eyes away.

The other one flicks his cigarette at me, too.

I think they see in me something they despise. They might see themselves, the way I see myself in them, too. It's why I'm here, maybe, not just in the Cass tonight, where I've apparently come only to get cigarettes flicked at me, but in Detroit in general, returning time and again to the center of my own parable.

I might be here solely to enter the darkness and walk through it.

CARRYING GUNS

T he next night I have another three-hour dinner with Erica and her dad, this time at the Red Cedar Grill, outside Okemos. Erica's dad again records the entire conversation, I think, through an earpiece hanging out of his shirt, connected to his cell phone's voice memo application. Erica confirms everything Chris had told me earlier.

When I ask her about her mother's boyfriend, she says, "I'm not sure about all of that. I'll have to ask her." But I sense that she's either being evasive or placating me, or it's just too emotional of a thing for her to contemplate at the moment. It's possible, too, that she doesn't remember.

I'm troubled by Gordy, the boyfriend, as there's substantial reason to believe that all four of the known OCCK victims were connected somewhere along the way with the case's most viable suspects. Mark Stebbins had just left a party that John was attending. Both Jill Robinson and Timothy King were connected to John McKinney Sr. via the Coffey residence. Kristine Mihelich's mother tended bar where both John and Christopher Busch were known to frequent.

Those suspects were not, to my eye, suspect due to their connection with the families. Those connections to the families only came to light after the men became suspects.

When I mention this to Erica and her dad, they nod their heads because they already know that. They don't understand how the details of things are piecing together, but they are convinced they're being lied to, which is like knowing everything at once and nothing at all.

Maybe that's why Erica is holding back from me. Maybe that's why her dad carries a gun, records our conversations, drives a truck you could roll through concrete in.

THE FRIDAY BEFORE I leave Detroit, I have coffee with Paula to say good-bye. We're at a chain coffee shop off Orchard Lake Road. I'm wearing my black combat boots, black jeans, and a black T-shirt.

"Wow," she laughs. "Who's the serial killer now?"

I try to laugh it off. There's another light bruise on my cheekbone that I tried to cover with a thirty-minute suntan before meeting her.

I know that something inside me has changed over the past six weeks. I'm unshaven and lonely, but that's the constant; Paula is sensing something in my eyes that maybe the apparel simply frames.

I tell her how good it's been to see her while I've been in town, to reconnect. When we talk about my dad, I tell Paula I got a bad feeling when he rubbed my daughter's shoulder at the Tigers game.

I tell her, "I'm territorial, I guess. I don't want him touching her."

HE COMES HERE, TOO

I take a detour on my drive home past the Evergreen Plaza Shopping Center and stop at the house I grew up in. Parking next to the curb that I used to spend summers sharpening wooden Popsicle sticks on, I get out and knock on the front door but nobody answers.

I walk around to the back where the brick-lined patio my father used to lift weights on has been torn out of the dirt and replaced with a concrete pad. The grass I burned down has gone to weed. In a far corner there's a swing set that wasn't there years ago, but it's as beat-to-hell as the one my father gave us.

I step onto the concrete patio and remember the girl named Jenny down the street from us, how we made wreaths from dandelions one summer, placed them on our heads in the grass beside this very spot, and married one another with the burn of sunlight in our hair. I remember not knowing how to tell Jenny anything about my family life but how the enmity inside my home was calmed by my ability to curl up inside Jenny's eyes and rest there faithfully in the harder moments. I couldn't have known I'd spend most of my adult life looking for that in somebody again. I drove by Jenny's house on my way into the neighborhood and there was a foreclosure sticker on the window and the inside of the house was like a box of darkness behind broken curtain rods.

I walk around to the front of my old house and knock on the door again and stand there, and when I'm about to leave, a black man in a tight shirt answers.

He locks the screen door with thinning fingers and says through the meshing, "You want something in my backyard?"

"I used to live here," I say.

"I know it," he says. "You look just like your old man."

Then we stare at each other, and I can feel the heat on the back of my neck and I look at the screen door and can tell that it hasn't been changed since all those years ago, since I was a kid, just like the entryway to Tim's home hasn't been altered, either.

I have returned, after all, and I recognize my place.

I look back at the man and his eyes are wide open and brown when he adds, "Pretty sure he comes here, too, you know."

I SPEND THE entire weekend in my hotel room, the curtains drawn, the privacy sign hung outside my door. I've turned off the ringer on both my cell and the room phone. At night a cube of red light blinks periodically, telling me a call is coming through, but I don't answer.

A few days later I drive to the Oak Park police station in the suburb south of Berkley. I haven't eaten. Inside the waiting area, I can smell the buildup of must and rankness from decades of crime shuffling through this space.

Behind a window, two black women are laughing at a joke. I'm wearing my suit because I'm doing last-minute research in a few office buildings where I think dressing sharply will work to my favor, but I'm white as the day is long in here.

They stop laughing when they see me.

"What you need, honey?" one of the women says. She has big hair curled into a huge puff around her head, the way my grandmother used to. She's pretty, and I can smell her perfume.

"I need to FOIA a case," I said. "I'm looking for a file going back to the seventies."

She hands me a form. I stare at it.

"Relationship to the case?" she says.

I look up at her. Her eyes are like toffee, waiting for me to answer. I look back down at the paper and start filling out the dates.

"It's my father," I say.

I believe that he has a file, one that I've never seen, but I want to know what's in it.

• • •

MY LAST MORNING in town, I have breakfast with Teresa in a diner. She'd been leaving me messages when I hadn't answered my cell. Now we order eggs and toast and bacon and coffee. I don't eat much of mine. We're mostly silent. Teresa reaches across the table and holds on to my hand. Her skin is soft and reminds me of my mother's.

She says after a while, "I don't think you're capable of falling in love with me."

I don't say anything.

She doesn't change the pressure on my hand when she says, "You might have become cold inside."

What I want to tell her is that even as a boy I knew how small my mother was in the hands of men like my father.

I want to say: The way a bag fills up with air, is carried away—that was the distance between myself and what I could do to save her.

ELLIE

I stop at a diner near Ellic's on my way to the airport that evening. She's in a booth in the back, pouring sugar into her coffee, when I see her for the first time in a year.

She looks up at me and sets the sugar down. Her skin is pale, her hair is unwashed, and her eyes have dark rings around them. Her lips looked dehydrated and cracked from twenty feet away when I come up to her.

"Thanks for calling," she says. Her voice has a tremor to it; her eyes are like black pools I could step inside.

I sit down on Ellie's side of the booth and push up beside her. We're silent at first, and then my shoulders are touching hers when I say, "I FOIA'd my own dad today."

We just sit there for a while, and she puts her hand beneath my hairline and touches me and holds her fingers to my skin and sweeps her hand behind my hair and allows for the waitress to walk by before she says, "Why?"

I don't say anything at first and then I know that I can't tell Ellie the whole story because my father's story, remarkably, is still his own, but after a while I tell her simply, "Because he deserved it, I guess."

I glide Ellie's spoon from the table and I'm squeezing it, and then an airplane cuts through the approaching dusk outside the diner window when I add, "Because he wasn't just pulled over randomly back then."

I can feel the edges of the spoon digging into the bones of my palm where I'm squeezing it when Ellie says to me, "Your father isn't the Oakland County Child Killer, Jason," and I know that, of course, but goddamn if I don't want to bury him for the fear in me that still trembles from the inside out all these years later.

She takes the spoon from my hand and puts her own hand where the spoon had been, and I bend into her lap. I curl into Ellie, pushing her to the back of that booth until I can't push anymore.

Ellie places her hands across my shoulders, and I am a small thing held by her for however long it will last, and if the people in the diner are looking I don't know, and I can hear another plane cutting through the coming darkness outside and I can smell the leather in Ellie's coat and feel the warmth of her hands soothing across my back and I hope it lasts a long time and I know that it can't, and I never see her again after that.

4:00 A.M.

We live out the consequences of our betrayals, usually not with precision, but with a great amount of estimation from the gods as to what our punishment should be. It's never going to be exactly an eye for an eye, but you can bet your ass it will hit you in the same genre of hurt.

When I got back to Idaho from Detroit, I was still tweaking from everything I'd learned about the case, but something was wrong in my home now, too. I spent a week showering my kids with affection, overwhelming them, rejoicing in them ad nauseam, but the emotional knickknacks were out of place on the shelves of my relationship with my wife. She spent a lot of time in silence. I spent my own amount of time analyzing that silence.

I'd been emotionally unfaithful with Teresa, maybe even fallen for Ellie in those last moments again, but I'd walked away from Detroit and come home to my kids and maybe even to my wife in many ways, if not physically. I was ready to do anything to keep my family together. The more impossible that seemed, the harder I fought, and the more hopeless I became. What I knew of my wife's affair—the knowledge blossoming in me at the time but without proof yet—and of my own transgressions, too, was enough to know that we couldn't turn back, but the uncertainty of what that meant for our kids was terrifying to me, and I raged within that terror.

One night I stood in the street out front of my neighbor's house at four in the morning, my own front door left open behind me and allowing the cold air in. I was barefoot, in only my pajama bottoms, twenty yards from the man's doorway. I wanted to cut him in the fucking neck, but underneath that, I knew, was my father punching my brother so hard it frightened me my whole life. Underneath all of my anger at the man in front of me in the darkness of that street was my anger at the man behind me in the darkness of four decades of fear, of rage against manipulation by my father, who had prevented me, I thought, from knowing love, from being able to give or receive honesty, from allowing myself to be whole or to live healthily.

I had a steak knife from our kitchen in my hand on the street that night. I saw it plunging into my neighbor's heart and I saw it plunging into my own afterward. I imagined my face dropping into the leaves of his yard, the last remnants of autumn dithering even in darkness from the big maple that cornered his property.

What held me from violence, what kept me from murder or my own suicide, was that each of us had children of our own, whom I would never leave or betray, not even his. There were young ones yet, lucky enough to be remembered by more than news clippings and aerial photos or footprints in the blood or snow, or in the leaves like an ellipsis leading to an early end.

ONE DAY IN November, after dropping off my kids at school, I sat a red light until it turned green and the cars were honking behind me. Out of nowhere, I became so insanely angry again. By the time I got home, the rage had taken over my body in a way I'd only seen happen to my father.

I parked my car crookedly in the driveway and kicked through the back door, storming around. My wife was still asleep and I shouted at her to get out of bed. I broke things against the walls, a vase that splattered into pieces like spring ice, a few picture frames that splintered at their corners, sending shards of glass careening across the room. I screamed at the top of my lungs like exorcising a demon. I broke what we had and more, it seemed.

My wife removed herself to a corner of the living room, curling away from me on a couch with her eyes alert, her body frozen into position while the various objects we'd collected over the years soared by and exploded into fragments against the walls we'd painted together after weeks of picking out colors.

Looking back, she was as my mother in that moment, and I was as my father. Hadn't I been fated to repeat that dynamic of violence after all?

When my wife finally confessed to her affair, I did not feel any relief whatsoever. There was no metaphorical releasing of the pressure cooker, no steam pouring out and emptying my burden of worry and suspicion, no draining of the pain of not knowing. I made my way into another room and shut the door.

I crumpled onto myself on the floor, shaking. Decades of pain came back to me. I was scared and alone again, afraid of what might become of my life, afraid of my kids disappearing from my arms that had held them so tightly for so long.

By December, my neighbor and my wife were hanging Christmas lights together at her rented house a few miles away, and I'd put a "For Sale" sign in the front yard of the home we'd built from the concrete up.

THE BERKLEY WITNESS

A few weeks after my meltdown, I get a return call from the Berkley Witness, Sebastian. Most of my house is packed up in boxes, so I sit on the floor in an empty room and set up my recorder. We speak for two hours.

It was Christmas Break, 1977, Sebastian tells me. He was nine years old.

The snow was falling, he says. He wanted to ride the new bicycle he'd gotten for Christmas, but his mom wouldn't allow it. Sebastian's mom was single and worked hard to provide for him, but she had a week off and they'd been looking forward to spending time together.

She worked at a bar on 6 Mile in Detroit. During a snowfall one afternoon, Sebastian's mom got called in to work and Sebastian used her absence from the home as an opportunity to take off on his new bike to a vacant lot where he cruised around in the snow.

Afterward, he rode down 12 Mile to the 7-Eleven store. As he pulled up, a young girl holding a bag containing what he could see was a magazine and a candy bar was walking toward a car.

Sebastian caught the girl's eye. Showing off for her on his new bike, he did a spinout in the snow. When he looked back at the girl, a cop was walking out of the 7-Eleven in full uniform behind her. Sebastian recognized the cop from the neighborhood.

Sebastian got worried that the cop, whom he assumed had recognized him, too, might rat on Sebastian for riding his new bicycle against his mother's wishes. Sebastian went home, cleaned off his bike, and hoped for the best.

A couple of days later Sebastian saw the girl's picture in the newspaper saying she'd been kidnapped. Her name was listed as Kristine Mihelich.

Sebastian, still afraid of getting into trouble for riding his new bicycle through the snow, said nothing to his mother about seeing the girl at the 7-Eleven. He did, however, tell me that he'd telephoned the OCCK hotline listed in the newspaper. The woman who took Sebastian's call mistook him as a prankster. She threatened to come to his house. Sebastian did not call again.

At school, after Christmas break was over, Sebastian told his art teacher what he'd seen at the 7-Eleven, the girl from the news getting into a cop car before disappearing. The art teacher thought Sebastian was making things up. After Timothy King went missing, Sebastian reiterated his story at school, saying, "I swear I saw that girl Kristine." The next morning Timothy King turned up dead, and Sebastian's story was reported up the chain. A day later, Sebastian says, two cops showed up at his school.

The two cops, Sebastian said, terrified him. They took Sebastian into a vacant classroom and accused him of lying. When Sebastian persisted, one responded by forcing Sebastian's head onto a desk and telling him, "Change your story."

Sebastian says that the second cop got close to his face, within inches, and added, "Those guys are killers. Forget you saw anything. They will cut down your whole family tree." The cops left Sebastian in the empty classroom, shaken. For a while after that, Sebastian slept under his bed.

During that following year, Sebastian met a girl and became close to her. Her dad was a cop. Sebastian and the girl were hanging out together when a police cruiser rolled by and Sebastian hid behind a tree. When the girl asked him why he seemed afraid, Sebastian asked if he could speak privately with her father. Curious about what was going on, the girl arranged a meeting.

That evening, Sebastian told the girl's father the story of his sighting of Kristine. He also told the girl's father about the cops scaring the shit out of him. The girl's father listened carefully, then gave Sebastian his business card.

He told Sebastian, "You stay home. Keep your doors locked."

Five days later the girl's father was shot twice in the chest with two different guns. It was labeled a suicide.

The girl's father was Flynn.

SAME NAME, SAME HOOD

In Sebastian's story, the deaths continue to pile up. In high school, Sebastian told a friend the story of seeing Kristine with a cop outside that 7-Eleven. He spoke of the school visit by the two cops, then of the later death of Flynn. This high school friend of Sebastian's called the state police and made a statement. It was a Wednesday when he made the call. By the weekend, he was found dead of an apparent suicide, having reportedly gassed himself in his parents' garage.

A year after that, Sebastian told the story to another friend. A day later, that boy got busted in school for marijuana possession. The cop who came to the school to investigate the incident was the same cop Sebastian had seen at the 7-Eleven with Kristine. One day later, Sebastian said, the boy who'd been busted for weed was found dead of a suicide, having also allegedly gassed himself in a car in the family garage.

When Sebastian was twenty-one and still living at home after years of depression, he confided in his mother about the threat level he'd felt from the cops that day at his school. His mother's response was that Sebastian should mind his own business, but to placate him she called the police and reported it. One of the cops who had come to Sebastian's school came with another to Sebastian's home intent on arresting him for harassment. With them was the cop Sebastian had seen with Kristine.

When he saw them in the driveway, Sebastian hid in the garage and locked the door. The cops pushed through the interior door somehow. They cornered Sebastian in his garage. They insisted on Sebastian leaving in a car with them, but Sebastian refused.

When they put their hands on Sebastian, a struggle ensued and they busted his face against a few cylinder heads that were lying on the garage floor.

The cop that'd been with Kristine, Sebastian says, kicked him in the face and then leaned down and grabbed his hair. "I saw you take that girl," Sebastian says he told the cop.

He could feel handcuffs tightening his arms behind his back. He could see his mother trying to dial for help from the doorway but somebody grabbed the phone from her hands, and then somebody else put a knee in Sebastian's back and pulled his head up, suffocating him with a hand until he was unconscious.

He says he remembers waking up on a gurney sometime later, tied four-point. He didn't know where he was. He slipped a hand out of his restraints and was punched in the head several times until blacking out again. He woke up at the Clinton Valley Center hospital with cuts in his wrists from the handcuffs, his teeth loosened from the blows, and his eyes temporarily blinded from broken blood vessels.

SEBASTIAN SAYS NO charges were ever filed by either side. He moved a few miles away to Oak Park, just outside of the Berkley PD's jurisdiction. He laid low for several years, working odd jobs, and sank further into depression.

Decades went by. Sebastian kept his mouth shut. Five years ago, he tells me, he moved back to his mother's house to take care of her. In 2009, no longer afraid of speaking out, he called the FBI.

Only six hours after his call to the FBI, he says, Detective Garry Gray of the original task force called him and asked about the story. Sebastian told him every detail and mentioned that he'd called Timothy's father, Barry King, as well. Gray told him to leave the King family alone.

After a few short breaths that suddenly turn into crying on his end of the line, Sebastian says to me, "There was another Sebastian in my hood when I was a kid. Looked just like me. Blond hair, same name, same hood." He tells me through his sobs that the cop he'd seen with

Kristine had hit the boy with a PD cruiser in June of 1977, the year Sebastian initially reported his story. "The guy is forty-three now," Sebastian adds. "Mentally deficient from that wreck, and been in a wheelchair his whole life. Even then, I knew that guy was supposed to be me."

A moment passes, and then he says, "This wasn't no abduction. Not like you think. She left the store and got into that car on her own like she'd already been in it before."

After a while, Sebastian says, "Almost everybody I've brought into this has been killed or their lives fucking destroyed." He's crying again, huge tears that I can hear across the phone line.

The 7-Eleven clerk from the day of Kristine's disappearance, Sebastian remembers, has also died, and also from an apparent suicide, although Sebastian doesn't remember when that occurred. A while ago, he tells me, he was working as a sandwich delivery driver, when he drove by the 7-Eleven and saw one of the cops who attacked him in the midst of a photo shoot related to this case. Sebastian had a Hungry Howie's sign atop his car, was still poor and depressed after decades, and kept driving.

When I run Sebastian's story by Cathy later, she tells me that Sebastian has also been in contact with a reporter in Detroit, an acquaintance of Cathy's. That reporter has looked into his narrative, Cathy says, and she believes she has confirmed at least parts of it. Cathy tells me she thinks the reporter has also confirmed Sebastian's medical records from the day he claims to have been pummeled into unconsciousness inside his mother's garage, but when I call Sebastian on my cell, he says that he himself wasn't able to obtain those records. Clinton Valley had told him their records didn't date that far back.

Cathy prints off a few emails she's exchanged with the reporter. I receive them from her in a manila file. I set them on the dash of my car and I drive out to a parking lot on the edge of the city and turn off my engine. I lock my car doors and read through the file of emails between Cathy and the reporter. I think again of all the ways we step away from the world and into our sadness, down the rabbit hole of narratives, and I imagine Sebastian in a fast-food-driven vehicle leading toward nowhere he'd likely have expected for his life.

CALL ME WHEN YOU'RE BETTER

I'm in the sauna at the gym downtown in my small city in Idaho, wearing a towel, my head resting against the wall. I'm listening to the drip of water onto rocks, the hiss of steam.

I haven't exercised in months. I've lost ten pounds over the winter. I've had sex with a woman other than my wife for the first time in years. She was the twenty-nine-year-old every forty-year-old man is supposed to pine after, and the act had all the inspiration of my seventh-worst game of bowling: not terrible, but certainly not the stuff of mythology.

I can feel myself losing interest in the world, shedding it like the weight, just letting it drip and peel away, like waiting for death to come, how you just sit there in the end and hope it happens without any more pain than you've already gotten used to.

By mid-February I've lost all memory of great chunks of the case. I've been told it's the depression coupled with poor nutrition leading to impaired cognitive function.

I have to go back and reexamine my notes before I can write, which I've gone months without doing, focusing on my kids instead but with tremendous effort. They can tell that I'm overcompensating again, trying to be the perfect dad, the way I used to be when I was fighting the urge to drink. My kids are hurting from the breakup and they don't need French toast as much as they need me to just sit with them, relax into the moment instead of asking every thirty seconds, "Do you need anything? Are you okay? Are you hungry? Can I make you food?"

My kids need a parent in me, but a partner in me, too, someone they can talk with, and I've been offering them a rapidly deteriorating hotel concierge instead as a substitute for lasting emotional leadership. But I'm not a concierge at a great hotel: It's like a Motel 6 around here and I'm the old guy whose only job is to refill the Lucite cereal dispensers.

When I step out of the sauna at the Y, I get on a scale for the first time in years and feel lightheaded when I look at the numbers. When I get dressed, I can see my ribs in the mirror. I lean over to pull my socks on, get dizzy, and have to sit down to finish changing.

I lie on my couch for two days. At some point I call a friend.

"You don't sound so good," he says. "Are you okay?"

I just sort of breathe out a "No" into the phone.

Neither of us speaks for twenty seconds. I'm sure he can hear me breathing and I can hear him typing on his laptop absentmindedly before he says, "Listen, man, just call me when you're better." I don't hear from him for another three months.

2:00 A.M.

Two weeks later, when my kids are gone, I force myself to make a pot roast, which I've bought with the food stamps I had to apply for, and I eat it for three days.

I start jogging and doing push-ups to prepare myself for hitting real weights in the gym again. Toward the end of that week, I feel stronger already. I've gained a few pounds back and started taking ginseng and ginkgo supplements. My head seems clearer.

But then two in the morning comes like a knife stuck under my chin one evening, adrenaline shooting through me. I tie on my running shoes, zip up a hoodie, and sprint the two miles between my rented house and the old home I'd failed at making a life in.

It's pitch-dark and once again I find myself in the street out in front of my neighbor's house, no knife in hand this time, but so furious with adrenaline that I could easily break through his front door, drag him into the street, and cut through his neck without even a weapon, with just my fingers.

I am so unhinged right now. I know it and I don't care. And now I have my strength back to go with it.

The streetlamp cuts across me the way it used to cut across the neighbor's car pulling up after a long night hidden away at a bar or hotel room or wherever he was with my wife. It cuts across me the way a knife would cut across the screen on his window and allow my entry into his home, as he had metaphorically entered mine, during all the seasons I imagine I'll still want to enter it but can't, knowing that violence removes both the victim and perpetrator equally from those that love them.

My father's fists, I imagine, would have punched a hole through this man's teeth, though—would've done it months ago if the decades had been reversed. I can see my father's hands dragging this man into a welding shop somewhere and keeping him with chains and a D ring, clenched to the floor.

Certainly I want to do the same thing, yet I also understand in this moment that my own power over the situation must come from somewhere else, from my grasp on the OCCK case, which is all I have—putting a bullet to the temple of these crimes might feel the same as putting a bullet to the head of the man who came into my house.

They have become the same being, the murderer on one hand, and the adulterer on the other. Although I, in turn, have become some version of my father at his worst—I am a predator now—I can use my strengths to cull not the weakest from the pack but the most insidious among us.

CLOWN

It's early summer. I've been lifting weights and eating right. I've gained back ten pounds of muscle, which I'll soon lose again, but right now I'm in better shape than ninety percent of adult males my age, and my kids and I have settled into a routine.

A mysterious man, using the pseudonym "Bob" and speaking only through an attorney he acquired in Detroit, has come forward to report intimate knowledge of the case. His claims are reminiscent of my own: that multiple perpetrators were involved in the killings, that a cop was possibly central to a cover-up, and that there were possibly more than four kids killed by the entities referred to collectively as the OCCK.

Bob, through his attorney Paul Hughes, announces a press conference slated for the coming weeks. I immediately get emails from strangers who have been following my work on the case, asking me if I am Bob. I had received a few small grants to continue my work, with subsequent news articles mentioning me, so I guess some readers made a connection that wasn't there. I don't know how people find my email address, but it's not too difficult to find most things if a person is motivated. This keeps me on edge.

I send an email to Paul Hughes, requesting an interview with the mystery man he represents, and Hughes forwards my email request to Bob.

Bob, in turn, responds, via Mr. Hughes. In his email, Bob has turned down my request for an interview, but instead of Mr. Hughes simply relaying that message to me, or pasting the relevant portions of Bob's response in quotes, he forwards Bob's entire email.

In the forward sent to me by Mr. Hughes, Bob wrote, "If *you* want to speak with him, you are more than welcome. But not me. I'd rather kill myself first. Hope you get what I think of this clown."

I'm the clown in this scenario.

I would stew about him calling me a clown but I don't worry about that, because underneath his signature, as a postscript, is a series of questions overriding any annoyance I might momentarily feel. Bob has addressed the following questions to Hughes:

1. Did you hear anything back from Danto's daughter?
2. Did the State Police get served?
3. Did you copy and delete emails?

I'm sitting at my dining table, where I write, when I read the email. My daughter is in her room playing records. My son is out back shooting an arrow through a box. I stand up to watch him out the screen window. He's pretty good at it, but all I can think is, *Danto?*

DR. DANTO

After Kristine's body was found on Bruce Lane, there was a lot of public speculation about Dr. Bruce Danto's involvement in the killings. Many thought the area psychiatrist was guilty of the crimes. More believed in a theory that the serial killer was lassoing Danto's reputation into the mix, due to Danto's academic studies on violence. Danto was an easy target for the obsessions of a killer, it was thought, and by entangling him with the OCCK case, maybe the killer was carving out a fast track to even greater celebrity than he'd already acquired with the murders themselves. The killer was making himself legendary, like the great serial killers before him, was the thinking at the time. The celebrity being branded equally fast, however, might have been Danto's.

After the body was found on a street bearing his name, Danto's smarmy intellectual-sitting-in-a-chair photo was blasted repeatedly throughout the papers and on television as the good doctor took interview after interview from reporters and hair-sprayed frontmen with only half of Danto's intellect. The media came to him like ants, and he fed them their sugar in the form of sound bites, much of it seemingly in service to boosting his own reputation as a psychiatrist of high position and caliber.

Shortly after Danto's fame began to blossom, he called the PD to report a mysterious package that had been sent to his office containing a typed, two-page letter from a man claiming to be the Oakland County Child Killer's roommate, begging for help. The letter, grammatically disastrous and in chopped syntax, read, verbatim:

DR. DANTO

I AM DSPERITE AND NEARLY GONE CRAZY AND HAVNT GOT NO PLACE LEFT TO TURN. I AM GOING TO COMIT SUICIDE IF YOU CANT HELP ME. PLEASE DONT GIVE UP THE KILLER TO THE POLICE. YOU MUST HELP ME AS THERE IS NO ONE ELSE I CANT TURN TO. THIS IS FOR REAL I KNOW WHO THE KILLER IS, I LIVE WITH HIM I AM HIS SLAVE. HE WHIPS ME AND BEATS ME ALL THE TIME. AND HE WILL KILL ME IF HE FINDS OUT THAT I HAVE WRITTEN THIS LETTER. I HAVE BEEN WITH HIM IN HIS CAR WHEN WE GO OUT LOOKING FOR BOYS BUT I SWEAR I HAVE NEVER NEVER NEVER BEEN WITH HIM WHEN HE PICKS UP THE ONES HE KILLSED BUT I

307

AMIN   IT IN IT SO DEEP I AM JUST AS
JUILTY TO THE LAW AS HE IS I STAYED
WITH THEM HERE HERE   RIGHT HERE
IN OUR APARTMENT DURING THE DAY
WHILE HE IS WORKING. THAT MAKES
ME JUST AS GUILTY. AND NO ONE CAN
HEAR THEM AS THEY GAGGED ALL THE
TIME. YOU KNOW HE BRINGS THEM
IN STUFFED INCLOTHES HAMPER NO
ONE HERE KNOWS THE DIFFERENCES.
YOU   KEEP SAYING OAKLNAD
COUNTY NOT TRUE. HE HAS DELIVERY
ROUT IN OAKLAND AND BIRMINGHAM
PLACES BUT WE LIVE IN DETROIT.
YOU WANT TO KNOW PEOPLE IN
THIS   BUILDING? PIMPS AND
HOOKERS AND FAGS, YOU NAME IT.
LIKE ON GREMLIN HE HAD IT SURE
GRIMLIN UNTIL LAST BOY BUT NO
ONE STOPS HIM IN DETROIT. HE JUNK
IT OUT IN OHIO TO NEVER BE FOUND
EVER. I TELL YOU WHAT MAKES HIM
DO IT IT VIETNAM, WE WERE THERE
TOGETHER, FRANK AND ME, OH FRANK
NOT HIS REAL NAME I CALL HIM THAT
HERE. NAM SCREW UP YOUR MIND DOC,
IT GOTTA BE FUCKIN NAM. YOU EVER
BE OVER THERE? ITWOULD SCREW UP
YOUR MINDTOO. TELL YOU SOMETHING
ELSE HE KILLED LOTS OF LITTLE KIDS

THEN WITH MEDALS FOR IT. BURNED THEM TO DEATH BOMBED THEM WITH NAPALM IT'S REAL BECAUTIFUL THERE DOC. HE WANTS THE RICH PEOPLE LIKE PEOPLE IN BIRMINGHAM TO SUFFER LIKE ALL OF US SUFFERED TO GET NOTHING BACK FOR WHAT WE DID FOR OUR COUNTRY. HES NOT A MONSTER LIKE YOU THINK HE RALLY LOVES CHILDREN ESPECIALLY THAT LITTLE GIRL FOR 3 WEEKS NOT DOING IT BECUASE HATES CHILDRENS BUT DOING IT BECAUSE HATES EVERYBODY ELSE OUT THERE AND THIS BE HIS WAY TO GET EVEN AND GET BACK AT EVERYBODY.

BUT I CANNOT DO IT ANY MORE HE SAYS HE WONTS BUT I JUST KNOW HE IS GOING TO KILL SOME MORE. I SWEAR I HAD NO IDEA NO IDEA HE GOING TO KIL THAT FIRST LITTLE BOY THE ONE WITH BLOND COLRD HAIR. I SHOULDN8T EVER NEVER HELPED BUT TRAPPED TOO LATE HELPED HIM STAY UNCAUGHT, I AM JUST AS GUILTY AS HE IS. I CANT GO ON LIKE THIS I FELL I FEEL LIKE TO DIE.

I WILL TURN HIM IN IF YOU WILL SE SWEARNTO HELP ME I DONT WANT ANY OF REWARD I AM SO AFRAID IF I TURN HIM IN I BE KILLED OR DO FOREVER TO

JAIL FOR WHAT SOMETHING I DIDN8T
WANT TO OR DIDN'T START. IF YOU BE
REAL DOCTOR YOU MUST HELP ME.
IF YOU PROMISE AND WHAT REALLY
PROMISE THAT YOU NOT PUNISH
ME LIKE YOU CALL IT IMMUNITY I
MEETING WITH YOU THIS SUNDAY
NIGHT, I SWEAR, I SWEAR I TELL YOU
ALL OF IT EVERYTHING I HAVE TO
TELL SOMEONE HAVE TO TELL SOME-
ONE. PLEASE PLEASE PLEASE NOT
PRINT THIS IN PAPER HE FRANK KILL
ME. I AM HIS SLAVE AND HE OWNS ME
LIKE WHATEVER HE WANTS ALMOST
KILLED ME ONCE. I BE ONLY ONE ALIVE
KNOW IT HIM. NOBOYD ELSE KNOW. I
SO SCARED ALL THE TIME POLICEMAN
COME TO DOOR NEVER HAPPEN. HE SAY
WE NEVER BE CAUGHT BY I AM SCARED
TO DIE. I BE GUILTY TOO. I NOT GE BE
CALL YOU ARAID POLICE TRACE ALL
YOUR CALLS BACK TO HERE. BUT IF
YOU WILL ONLUY PLEASE PLEASE HELP
ME HELP ME AND PROMISE ME NOT
TO GO TO JAIL IN WRITING I TELL YOU
ALL OF IT EVERYTHING EVERYTHING
AND IT ALL BE OVER. I NEVER NEVER
WANT IT TO BE LIKE HTIS WITH
LITTLE   CHILDREN DEAD. IF YOU WILL
HELP ME PLEASE PLEASE. THERE BE NO

TOHER HOPE. YOU TELL ME IT BE ALL RIGHT WITH CODE IN SUNDAY PAPERS, THIS SUNDAY, NEWS FREEPRESS. YOU DO LIKE OTHER LETTER YOU WRITE ON FRONT PAGE OF PAPERS, THIS SUNDAY, IT BE TO SAY, WEATHER BEUAU SAY TREES TO BLOOM IN 3 WEEKS—YOU UNDERSTAND WHAT I TO SAY TO YOU, IT BE CODE I KNOW YOU GET MY LETTER AND YOU UNDERSTAND. YOU MAKE IT TO SAY TREES TO BLOOM IN 3 WEEKS, I KNOW YOU GET MY LETTER AND UNDERSTDNA. IT MEAN I CAN TRUST YOU, I SET UP MEETING WITH YOU, NO MORE LITTLE CHILDRENS DIE. PLEASE HELP ME PLEASE. I FEEL SO BAD LIKE GARBAGE NOT DESERVE TO LIVE ANYMORE. MAYBE I KILL SELF FIRST MUST GET OUT OF THIS SOME WAY. PLEASE HELP ME.

I SINGND ALLEN

The PD went to Danto's office, retrieved the letter, and began working with Dr. Danto to disseminate the information and lure the mysterious "Allen" out of hiding.

Danto, who had received a small amount of police training ancillary to his studies on violence, seemed overly eager. He requested a permit to carry a pistol in his boot. This was denied. He volunteered to have his home telephone tapped in anticipation of further contact.

A notice about the trees blooming in three weeks, per Allen's request, was placed in the Sunday paper by the police. The morning the paper came out, Danto received a phone call at home, spoken in chopped English like the letter. The call was recorded. Allen's end of the conversation follows:

I want [unintelligible] immunity. I want it by tomorrow night I mean tomorrow 9:00 [unintelligible]. You be at Seven Mile and Woodward you know where Pony Cart Bar, you listen to me this only time I'm calling you [unintelligible]. You want hang up, you hang up [unintelligible] but this is what I'm telling you [pause]. You be Pony Cart bar tomorrow night at 9:00 with letter from governor of Michigan giving me total immunity in return I give you Polaroid pictures proving he kill them [pause]. That's all I'm going to say [pause]. You be there [pause]. This is a bar [pause]. Jesus [unintelligible]. Seven Mile near Woodward [pause]. Be there [unintelligible]. Pony Cart Bar [pause]. You be there, no police [pause]. I know everybody in there [long pause]. You no bring police you be there by

312

yourself [pause]. You be there 9:00 tomorrow [pause]. No it's a bar you stu [unintelligible]. You be there 9:00 tomorrow [pause]. You no bring police I prove he kill them. That's all I say.

The phone went dead after that. The PD buried a microphone in Danto's chest hairs the next night and shoved him into the Pony Cart Bar like a blindfolded kid swinging at a piñata.

A detective, undercover as a student, sat at a table pretending to read a textbook while Danto sat at the bar and waited for the mysterious correspondent to show up. Danto was talkative with the bartender, overacting. Meanwhile, a man with broken English approached the undercover detective, Jerry Tobias, and offered to buy him a drink. The Pony Cart was a gay bar, and the detective got flustered. He sent his solicitor packing.

Allen never came forward that evening, or ever again. In retrospect, the PD speculated that the man offering their cop a drink must have been the man they'd been waiting on, testing to see if Tobias was a cop or a regular patron. It was a missed opportunity, lost because Tobias couldn't fit in.

THE "ALLEN" STORY is suspect to me, however. The initial letter presents not just broken

English but the disjointed, nearly illiterate, almost psychotic thinking of a person of extremely low IQ, yet simultaneously the letter writer was smart enough to track down a psychiatrist with a specialized interest in violent perpetrators instead of just shooting off his letter to the police or press, which would have been much easier.

In the letter, he requests "like you call it immunity," which suggests a certain naïveté about the process of being granted such things; but then, in his phone call to Danto, he is very forthright about requesting immunity by the governor himself, suggesting a more educated understanding of the system.

Possibly more interesting than Allen is Danto's involvement. When the letter writer refers to his roommate's Gremlin being junked "out in Ohio to never be found ever," I remember Danto's own connection to Ohio, where he'd once talked a serial killer into giving himself up. I remember that Ted Lamborgine was known to have spent time in Ohio, too, trolling for hitchhikers. Another dead girl, Jane Allen, had been found in a river down there, her abduction and murder having similarities to the OCCK crimes—there was often speculation that the Allen murder was related.

Danto had too casually strolled into the largest homicide investigation on the planet at that time, turning up hot evidence in the form of an anonymous letter, requesting a boot gun, loitering around task force headquarters, and going over evidence with the PD—then eventually showing up in an email accidentally sent to me.

THE DRY CLEANER

I come across a notation in the Tommy McIntyre book *Wolf in Sheep's Clothing*. McIntyre was a fine, respectable reporter in the Detroit area during the 1970s and 1980s, with police department inroads that, I've come to believe, undermined his objectivity about those he trusted. The book seems slanted toward a thesis of praise for the investigation and without diligent inquiry, although there is indeed some important information contained in its pages, including the content of the "Allen" letter and telephone call. The book also includes a transcript of a letter from the FBI lab in D.C. to their field office in Detroit, disseminating that letter and call. The portions of the Allen letter stating that the OCCK had carted his victims home in a clothes hamper and had a delivery route of some sort seemed especially interesting to the FBI analyst, as indicated below:

It is noted that all of the victims were thoroughly cleaned with "Phisohex," a product which was taken off the market several years ago. Since this procedure would necessarily require a fairly large amount of this product, the possibility exists that the individual involved in these killings is employed by a company . . . laundry, etc. . . . that would have used this product in large quantities . . .

If the FBI believed in the myth of the Phisohex-scrubbed bodies, then it did so based not on its own autopsy examinations but on reports pushed up the chain to it.

If I start from scratch with the Phisohex—ignoring what I know about the state of the bodies—I'd look at the dry-cleaning establishment next to Hunter-Maple Pharmacy, whose parking lot Timothy King disappeared from. When I followed that lead, I found reports of sexual misconduct from one of the dry cleaner's employees.

As it happens, that employee was friends with Christopher Busch.

LAWSON AND LAMBORGINE

Richard Lawson, aka Coyote Negro Lawson, offender #598802, a white male standing six feet five inches tall and weighing 210 pounds, passed quietly away a few months before my phone call with Chris King in which King reminded me that nobody dead can testify.

We'd both assumed Lawson was still behind bars, yet his corpse was already decomposing while we'd had our talk.

Lawson lived a long life, mostly as a free man and without a known murder attempt on his person. At the age of sixty-six, he'd served only six and a half years of the life sentence handed down to him for the killing of the cabbie, a murder he'd committed seventeen years prior to his sentencing.

THEODORE LAMBORGINE, AKA Ted Orr, is still alive, serving out his life sentence on fourteen convictions for criminal sexual conduct (CSC), twelve of them stemming from the summer of 1976, only months before the first OCCK murder.

There are two additional charges of CSC with a person under thirteen against Lamborgine. The date of offense is listed as December 31, 1980.

Only three years after the last known OCCK murder.

On a holiday.

During the winter months.

TRUST

On September 18, 1976, seven months after Mark Stebbins was murdered and two months before Jill Robinson was murdered, Francis Shelden of Fox Island began to establish a revocable living trust, organized in the British Virgin Islands, to control the majority of his relatively liquid assets.

The Trust Company of the Virgin Islands, Ltd., held approximately 2.5 million 1970s dollars, some of it as cash but mostly as shares of marketable securities in twenty-four corporations. Shelden's investments were in oil, booze, newspapers, mining, transportation, chemicals, banks, and manufacturing, with the exception of his 40,000 shares in the entity known as North Fox Island Company.

Shelden's wealth was far greater than what the trust controlled, but he was in a hurry to abscond with those funds that could be accessed easiest, as two months prior he'd received a call from Dyer Grossman saying that Gerald Richards, the gym teacher who had collaborated with Frank Shelden on child molestations, had been picked up by the PD. At Grossman's suggestion, Shelden contacted Adam Starchild, a specialist in offshore financial shelters. Francis Shelden had never met Starchild, but after a phone call to him in New Jersey, during which Starchild convinced Shelden of his expertise, Shelden removed his investment certificates from their safety-deposit box at a local bank and flew to Starchild for a covert meeting, his stock certificates in hand.

At Starchild's suggestion, a loan was obtained against some of the stocks. Two bank accounts were opened, each holding around $40,000, one account for Shelden and one for Starchild as payment for the ongoing administration of Shelden's account.

Shelden first fled to Europe via Canada. Later, at a meeting at the Shelden family home in Antigua on September 28, 1976, the trust was signed into effect, with Starchild as legal administrator and Shelden reserving the right, via his attorney L. Bennett Young, to remove Starchild and replace him with a successor if needed. Shelden returned to Europe and, two months later, the MSP issued warrants for his arrest that would go unrequited.

In 1977, while Shelden was living in Amsterdam, he began to realize that Starchild had been skimming large amounts of money from the trust. By April of 1978, Shelden removed Starchild and appointed a new successor, Edward Brongersma, his attorney in Amsterdam who at one time was a member of the upper house of the Dutch senate and chairman of the judicial committee. Shelden had once again established the deep political connections he'd become accustomed to in the States.

Eighteen months later, in October of 1979, Shelden again transferred control of the trust, but this time back to the U.S., with L. Bennett Young and the Detroit Bank & Trust Company now serving as cotrustees. Shelden's brother, Alger Shelden Jr., eventually jumped into the mix as a coadministrator. Starchild, in frustration at being removed from the trust, illegally attempted to exercise his previous status as administrator and fraudulently replaced Shelden's choices of oversight with his own, forging paperwork and naming a disbarred New York lawyer (himself convicted of a 1975 cocaine smuggling conspiracy) as president and treasurer of the trust, as well as sole beneficiary of both bank accounts. The move allowed a temporary shift of funds back into Starchild's domain but was eventually overturned.

Shelden's status as a fugitive in Europe would, theoretically, prevent him from receiving financial transfers from the States. In practice, however, Alger, Young, and multiple others, all Americans and easily accessible by law enforcement, would be responsible for Shelden's continued survival as a predator of means and affiliation. Regardless of the nearly one million dollars Starchild had reportedly siphoned from the accounts, Shelden still lived high on the hog until his death and was not known to have returned to the U.S. since his initial flight, meaning that he was overseas prior to the final three known OCCK murders. He can therefore not be considered a suspect in the deaths of Jill Robinson, Kristine Mihelich, or Timothy King.

STARCHILD

By 1980, Adam Starchild was temporarily residing in a small house in a pasture outside of St. Petersburg, Florida. From his living room office, he ran an international financial bilking front known as Minerva Consulting Group, Inc. He was thirty-three years old and heavyset, and wore thick-framed, horn-rimmed glasses. He had business cards stating he was a member of the Hong Kong Chamber of Commerce. He had done time in both American and British prisons for mail fraud and forgery.

It had been four years since Francis Shelden had absconded, but, from his pasture in Florida, Starchild again surfaced as a man of mystery, this time with ties to U.S. representative Richard Kelly, one of nine congressmen implicated in an undercover FBI investigation, code-named Abscam, an entrapment scheme by the feds that eventually rooted out evidence of a culture of bribery and influence peddling among our highest public officials.

Starchild's involvement with Representative Kelly was murky, but not as murky as the con man's past. Born Malcolm Willis McConahy on September 20, 1946, in Minnesota, he faked his death sometime between the February of Mark Stebbins's murder and that following spring by submitting an obituary for himself to a New Jersey newspaper, mailed in from a location in Vermont, claiming an auto accident took his life in Minnesota.

In August, six months after the Stebbins murder and one month before Shelden fled the country, McConahy took the name Adam Aristotle Starchild. What Adam Starchild left behind as Malcolm McConahy was a history of arrests for sexual perversions, including possession of child pornography and multiple charges of indecency with a minor.

Court records in Milwaukee, Minneapolis, Washington, and New Jersey show McConahy to have been an avid litigant and prodigious writer of complaint letters to local politicians. He once sued President Nixon on a trumped-up accusation that was thrown out of court. McConahy even sued his own mother in an effort to extort $90,000 from her, in a case that was eventually settled by the estate after her death.

In 1968, at the age of twenty-two, McConahy was running a Milwaukee travel agency specializing in adventures for youth groups. That same year found McConahy facing the aforementioned sex charges. He fled the state in the middle of his sex trial, embarked on a letter-writing campaign denouncing American justice, and crossed the Atlantic.

In 1970, McConahy began his four years in a British prison on forgery charges. He was eventually deported in 1974 to face his pending charges in America, where he served out a brief stint at the federal penitentiary in Sandstone, Minnesota. Shortly after release from that prison, the OCCK killings started.

IN DECEMBER OF 2012, the Boy Scouts of America was compelled to release what is known as "the Perversion Files," naming the accused in over five thousand case reports of sexually related crimes and tracking internal correspondences related to decades of molestations that had been concealed to protect the puritanical image of Scouting in America.

Malcolm Willis McConahy is named in those Perversion Files as assistant scoutmaster of Troop 27 in Minneapolis, having confessed, while facing insurmountable evidence and personal testimony against him, to the sexual molestation of multiple boys in his care in 1965 at the age of nineteen.

THE MINERVA CONSULTING Group remained an umbrella organization for decades' worth of Adam Starchild's organized criminal business dealings, beginning with his relationship to drug and gun smuggling, then accelerating to stock inflation, and political influence and corruption during the Abscam days. In later years, Starchild made a hefty ancillary living self-publishing his how-to books on eluding the government, gaining multiple citizenships and dual passports, setting up non-traceable trusts, and remaining off the grid.

Secondary businesses in its last decade included the distribution of over a hundred trademarked gift products: shot glasses, back-scratchers, barbecues, bookmarks, baby toys, and all manner of other items imported cheaply and sold under monikers related to traditional American heroes (for example, the "Paul Bunyan Axe"). Nearly every application for trademark listed the address 4440 NW 73rd Avenue PTY-362, in Miami, Florida. Google Maps shows the location as a nondescript tract of industrial ware-houses. Multiple searches for the Minerva group cite Adam Starchild as director and president, with one Javier E. Castano as vice president.

An online obituary shows Starchild to have passed away from tumor complications on September 20, 2006, and indeed most of his trademarks are listed as having been abandoned, with the notation of "DEAD" having been input by the U.S. Patent and Trademark Office for cause.

Castano remains listed with the company, yet other searches for Starchild list Castano as an alias for him. In fact, an obituary for Javier E. Castano says he died three years before Starchild. I contemplate whether Starchild could have faked his death again and be living under another assumed identity.

Not surprisingly, Starchild's obituary notes him as having been a member of MENSA, an organization whose entry is reserved for those with the highest two percent of IQs in the world. I confirm Starchild's membership with the MENSA organization and realize that Starchild, man of mystery, was no doubt brighter than every 1970s cop in Detroit, brighter than the Frank Sheldens of the world, and possibly brighter than anybody Starchild himself ever laid eyes on.

LeMANS

The snow was heavy and freshly fallen at the Kristine Mihelich drop site on Bruce Lane. The dead-end turnaround was banked with new buildup over the plow-pushed edges of the street. The vehicle that had been used to drop Kristine had backed into a snowbank before pulling away and left a rear bumper impression, which was identifiable as belonging to a 1973 Pontiac LeMans, Pontiac Tempest, or Buick Skylark—all of which looked nearly identical—with a damaged driver's-side back end and a crooked trailer hitch.

The ghost of this damaged vehicle continues to haunt insiders to the case. Contrary to the blue Gremlin, a Pontiac or Buick is the last thing anybody in the public thinks about when they recollect the Oakland County Child Killings; like nearly every other detail of relevance, it had been redacted from the official storyline.

The ghost vehicle was not just at Kristine Mihelich's drop site, either. A motorist identified a Pontiac LeMans or Tempest with driver's-side rear damage as a vehicle seen creeping along the shoulder of I-75 in the predawn hour just before Jill Robinson's body was found there. A witness places yet another LeMans at the Timothy King parking lot abduction site, stating that a suspicious-looking "older man" sat in the driver's side of the vehicle while a "young man" was outside talking to a boy with an orange skateboard: Timothy King. This would corroborate Chris King's conviction that the blue Gremlin wasn't the abduction vehicle because it was still in the parking lot in the hours after Timothy's abduction.

As well, evidence collected from the Mark Stebbins drop site is catalogued to include what investigators labeled "Pontiac debris." We do not know how long the rear damage to the Pontiac had existed before leaving its imprint at the Kristine site, but if this is indeed the same vehicle used in at least one stage of the crimes, either the abduction or the drop of the OCCK kids, then we can speculate that its damage occurred as it backed into the brick wall where Mark Stebbins was dumped, leaving behind the collected debris. It would have been in a hurry to dump the body, slamming into the wall.

A witness places a Pontiac in the parking lot where Mark Stebbins was found that same morning.

RETIRED POLICE LIEUTENANT Jack Kalbfleisch from the original investigation, who spends his time helping out the National Center for Missing and Exploited Children, has kept a file on the circumstantial and physical Pontiac evidence these thirty-five years and is convinced that it should have been a major focus of the investigation, both internally and publicly.

At Ray Anger's request in 2005, Kalbfleisch turned over his personal work on the case to supposedly help the investigation. The file contained multiple theories about the Pontiac and backed them with solid police work. Kalbfleisch waited patiently to learn Anger's thoughts about the file but never heard back. He sent several follow-ups via email but received no response.

IN APRIL OF 1977, the Timothy King parking lot witness was hypnotized by the FBI and recalled seeing Tim skateboarding on the evening of his abduction. This recall helped the FBI nail down composite sketches of the "older man" and "young man" associated with the LeMans in the parking lot. The sketches of the men were never released publicly and are redacted from the FOIA documents, but their existence supports at least one theory of multiple perpetrators that was never disseminated to the press.

It's a theory that allows for the blue Gremlin: the two men drive separately to the parking lot behind the Hunter-Maple Pharmacy, the younger man parks his car off to the side, gets out, snatches Timothy King, and then shoves him into the LeMans, which they all drive off in.

As a possibility, it's not fucking rocket science.

TWO GUNS, TWO GUYS

T he cop named Flynn, whom Chris King had brought to my attention, was found dead of a reported suicide just after midnight in a church parking lot. He'd bled out in a blue 1973 Buick.

A nun and a priest from the church reported two people parked in a blue vehicle in the darkness of that same spot three hours earlier.

Documents list the two guns discovered inside Flynn's vehicle as his own police-issue weapon and a .44-caliber that was registered to his partner and found on the passenger-side floor. No gunshot residue tests are indicated in official documents.

The date of Flynn's death was November 14, 1978: two gunshot wounds to the chest, two different guns, two people seen in his car, no residue reported on his hands.

Chris Busch was found dead on November 22, 1978: rifle shot to the forehead, his body tucked into bedsheets, no gunshot residue found.

But Busch had been rotting for an estimated four days before the body was discovered, which places his actual date of death only a handful of days after Flynn's.

ARCH SLOAN

I t's January again, 2013.

The grand juries have by now both convened
and come up empty, Cathy informs me over the
telephone, although a few weeks ago a reporter
in Detroit got ahead of the police and released
a story about a new suspect named Archibald
"Arch" Sloan, incarcerated since 1983 for sex
crimes against young boys. Like Christopher
Busch and Gregory Greene, although roughly ten
years older, Sloan had a long history of charges
against him, beginning with gross indecency
at the age of eighteen, progressing to rape and
sodomy by the time he was in his twenties.

Sloan, now white-haired and with a downturned
mouth and a neck gone predictably doughy
from aging in prison, was born in Pennsylvania
but raised in Detroit and went to high school at
Cooley High during the period my father was
there. When my father was a senior and Sloan
a sophomore, Sloan dropped out of school and
worked as a mechanic and tow truck operator. He
moved back to Pennsylvania for a while, did time
on his first sex charges, then returned to Detroit

in 1975 and worked at multiple service stations while residing in Southfield, just a few miles from the Mark Stebbins drop.

During the initial OCCK suspect sweep, Sloan was questioned due to his criminal history and proximity to the crimes. In fact, he was given a lie detector test and appeared to pass it—a test administered by Ralph Cabot, the same man whose tests of Busch and Greene were later reviewed and found faulty.

Regardless of Sloan's test results, his vehicle, a red 1966 Pontiac Bonneville, was processed for evidence. Hair and carpet fibers were collected and stored. Reportedly, human hairs were mislabeled as animal hairs until 2013, when the Michigan State Police submitted them for DNA testing.

The hairs in Arch Sloan's vehicle are a mitochondrial match to hairs found on Mark Stebbins and Timothy King. The Bonneville hairs match a single strand retrieved from the exterior clothing of Stebbins, a single strand on Timothy King's underpants, and a single strand found in Timothy King's nasal cavity.

While the hairs found in Sloan's vehicle are a match to those found on the bodies, they are not a DNA match to Sloan himself, it turns out, and they are not a DNA match to Gunnels, either. The hair in Sloan's Bonneville must have come from somebody else.

Equally tricky is that the Bonneville hairs are only a mitochondrial match to the hairs found on the bodies of the two boys. They are not a nuclear match, meaning the Bonneville hairs and the hairs found at autopsy, although their origins were likely related, may have originated from different people—brothers or cousins, for instance.

In 1983, Arch Sloan was living in a trailer at the abandoned Packard plant complex, a favorite among those now seeking what is becoming known as "ruin porn" in Detroit: the long, block-after-block stretches of monstrously oversized buildings shattered and infected by emptiness decades ago, like the Brewster-Douglass Housing Projects.

Living a troll's existence in his small trailer, Sloan would ply young boys with alcohol and then rape them amid the industrial vacancies. For those and related crimes, he is serving two life sentences, neither of them for murder. While Arch Sloan could point us in the right direction toward the OCCK, he has nothing to gain from doing so. He has clamped down in silence to finish out his time and whatever he can call a life now.

We can reasonably assume, however, that Sloan's era of chicken hawking in Detroit would have placed him in contact with Lawson and Lamborgine. We can also reasonably assume one degree of separation between the passenger in Sloan's '66 Bonneville and Vincent Gunnels, since transfer hairs from each were evidenced on the bodies. Finally, we can assume that Sloan, like Gunnels, was among the parties closest to the crimes.

THE LE ROSEY SCHOOL

L e Rosey, an exclusive boarding school in
Rolle, Switzerland, outside of Geneva, is
headquartered on a secluded educational compound comprising a fourteenth-century château
at the center of more modern buildings dotting
hardwoods and pastures. Le Rosey, catering
to the primary and secondary educations of the
wealthiest children in the world, is in fact the
most expensive private school in the world
at $113,000 per year, servicing students ages
seven to eighteen. The student-to-teacher ratio at
Le Rosey is five to one, and Le Rosey is the only
boarding school in the world to change campuses
seasonally. While the château grounds at Rolle
are appropriate for the extracurricular spring
and autumn activities offered at Le Rosey—
flying lessons, horseback riding, shooting—
during winter months, the entire student body
relocates to a group of chalets in the ski town of
Gstaad.

As a child, the shah of Iran attended Le Rosey.
So did Winston Churchill. So did King Albert II
of Belgium, King Fuad II of Egypt, ex–CIA

director Richard Helms, and King Juan Carlos I of Spain. Alexander, crown prince of Yugoslavia, went there, as did Ian Campbell, 12th Duke of Argyll; Prince Rainier of Monaco; Prince Edward, Duke of Kent; and Emanuele Filiberto, prince of Venice and Piedmont. The Rothschilds went to Le Rosey, as did the du Ponts, the Rockefellers, the Gettys, and the Heinz family. Le Rosey's children are the children of Middle Eastern oil tycoons, Japanese industrial lords, American tobacco kids, the sons of sheikhs and mustard barons, of Russian oligarchs and American movie royalty, the children of Greek shipping magnates and French champagne makers. Guillaume, Grand Duke of Luxembourg, went there. Hermon Hermon-Hodge, 3rd Baron Wyfold of the British House of Lords, went there.

Christopher Busch went to Le Rosey as well, for both grade school and high school. After his graduation from the twelfth grade, he stayed on briefly as an assistant instructor. When he returned to Michigan, he left his posh grade school behind but not the international network and closest relationships he had known as a boy, with those other sons of millionaires, billionaires, and gods.

COMMON DENOMINATORS

The woman who testified to the FBI of her father's involvement in a 1970s pedophile ring detailed multiple circumstantial links between Christopher Busch and the crimes she witnessed in her father's presence.

That the men she associated with her father would meet and exchange both boys and girls at a gravel pit aligns with what is known of a Greene-Busch gravel pit transfer point. That the schoolteacher remembered whom she believed to be a large bearded man of considerable power and influence also aligns (admittedly, even more circumstantially), and her assertion that the molestations and murders she'd witnessed had been captured on camera matches with what we can reasonably understand to be Christopher Busch's trafficking in pornography.

That the schoolteacher refused to report to state or local authorities about the incident, opting only to speak to the FBI due to what she believed was area police involvement in the crimes, corresponds with the mysterious cover-up of what is undoubtedly not Christopher Busch's suicide but

Christopher Busch's murder by any reasonable accounting of the evidence.

That Christopher Busch had one suitcase full of approximately 115 items of child pornography, including books, magazines, and films, and two other suitcases containing ligatures, drugs, and photographic evidence in his possession when arrested would indicate his involvement in a less spontaneous, primarily premeditated pursuit of sexual deviancy. He did in fact confess to child abduction fantasies and subsequently named the points of abduction of OCCK victims as his trolling grounds.

As now known via information received from Busch's parole officer, Christopher Busch had associates who frequented Frank Shelden's Fox Island. He also had associates linking him to Lawson and Lamborgine. That he was associated with Gunnels and Sloan, the two men whose mitochondrial DNA was found on the bodies of the victims, would reasonably imply that Christopher Busch was the greatest common denominator among the widest body of legitimate suspects.

That the Busch family's influence was powerful and wide and that its scope branched throughout a political structure built on industry is without challenge. That its scope could have extended into the influence of law enforcement as well cannot be reasonably ignored when taking into account the abandonment of crime scene protocol at the Busch residence (for example, in allowing Busch Sr. to maintain possession of the weapon that reportedly killed his son); the plea deal struck to allow Busch's sentencing of probation in contrast to the life sentence handed down to Greene for the same crimes; and the official polygraph found to have been faulty only decades later when reviewed by multiple independent polygraphers.

Christopher Busch's death being ruled as a suicide by rifle shot to the forehead, the ligatures in his closet, and the drawing of Mark Stebbins at the death scene are circumstantial. What is most relevant about the Busch death scene is the lack of blood spatter, the absence of gunshot residue, and the positioning of the body—still wrapped tightly in the bedsheets—being more indicative of a murder.

That the case opened on Christopher Busch's death was closed as a suicide prior to the receipt of any lab reports is also of note. That Christopher Busch's body was wrapped in his linens is suspect, as he could not likely shoot himself point-blank in the head and then wrap his arms in the bedsheets before dying. That the wrapping of his body likely happened postmortem, prior to discovery, is of great relevance to the unpacking of the scene.

That Christopher Busch owned and drove at

least one vehicle matching the description of at least one suspected vehicle is of note. That Christopher Busch was named in one of the earliest tips telephoned in to the task force, #369 of tens of thousands of tips to be called in, and that this tip on Busch would mysteriously be erased from voice recordings, is of note.

That the victim questioned in 2008 testified to having been forced into sexual activity with a boy whom he believed later to have been Timothy King, and that he further testified to having been shown a Polaroid picture of a boy he believed to be Timothy King tied up in the trunk of Christopher Busch's vehicle, is of note. That the victim testified to being present when Christopher Busch dropped Timothy King off at the home of Ted Lamborgine is of note.

That Ted Lamborgine refused to take a polygraph on the OCCK murders, opting for a life sentence instead of a plea deal reducing his sentence to fifteen years in exchange for the polygraph, is of note. That Ted Lamborgine's initial response when interrogated about involvement in the OCCK was "I've been forgiven" is of note. That when further interrogated about the OCCK, years later, and offered another opportunity to take a polygraph, Ted Lamborgine's statement to police was simply "I didn't do it" is of note, along with what would be a common deduction from this: that Lamborgine, while possibly not a participant in the murders, may have had intimate knowledge of the crimes, answering in a way that career criminals often do, in a language that circles and takes without giving back.

That Richard Lawson made statements to police indicating that Lamborgine showed him pornographic images of a child who resembled Timothy King, and that Lawson further claimed to be able to identify a man in the photograph with King but would not reveal a name unless bargaining for a deal (which was never offered), is also of note.

That the letter from the infamous "Allen," albeit unverified, also indicates the existence of Polaroid pictures of the crimes; that Helen Dagner says John spoke of Polaroid pictures of the crimes. That multiple victims of Busch's molestations indicated Polaroid pictures of the crimes; that Gregory Greene, when interrogated, indicated a packet of tinfoil-wrapped pedophilic Polaroid pictures buried in the snow beneath a downspout of his home; and that those pictures were acknowledged by police as recovered and catalogued but eventually "lost" is of note.

That the crimes of violent, sociopathic predators tend to progress in proportion to the predator's growing courage is known. That Gregory Greene abducted and sexually assaulted a boy anally, then suffocated him with a hand and choked him into unconsciousness before burning him with a cigarette and finally depositing the young boy's body on the grounds of a hospital in California, is known.

That Gregory Greene dumped the boy in plain sight out of regret peppered with hope that the boy might still be alive or could be brought back to life somehow is known, and that Greene subsequently telephoned the hospital to alert them of the boy's presence is known.

That, when arrested later in California, Gregory Greene was found to have a police-issue scanner and communications radio in his vehicle is known. That Gregory Greene had been working as a confidential narcotics informant with the Huntington Beach Police Department is now known.

That, as penalty for the charge of false imprisonment, attempted murder, and forty to fifty charges of child molestation, Gregory Greene served less than a year in a mental hospital and then was released to freedom in Michigan is known. That a year after his release the OCCK murders began and that the victims are believed to have been suffocated via burking and then dumped in plain sight is known.

That, after Greene's prison death in 1995 of an alleged heart attack while watching television at the age of forty-seven, Greene's brother testified to police that the house they grew up in with their ailing father had a secret room in the attic, handbuilt by Gregory Greene and concealed from the naked eye, which Greene had used to "keep and molest boys in," is reported in the documents and generally known by police.

That, on November 15, 1976, just over a month before Jill Robinson was abducted, a juvenile runaway report filed six days earlier was considered "cleared" when it was discovered that the boy had spent those six days at Gregory Greene's house, hidden in the concealed attic room while Greene was at work, and that no charges were filed against Greene, is known. That a victim in the molestation charges that finally put Greene away reported that, during oral copulation, Greene choked him by the neck until he passed out is known.

That Christopher Busch's younger cousin, also molested by Busch and Greene, stated that Busch was never violent with him, aside from the inherent violence of molestation, while Greene was frightening and always violent, is known.

That the victim who reported Greene to have choked him unconscious also reported statements Greene made about Busch choking and killing a boy in the woods is known; that, after Greene's death, his cellmate reported that Greene had claimed to have gotten away with killing four kids is also known.

That Gregory Greene named Busch as Mark Stebbins's killer is known; that he did so as an act of self-preservation under interrogation, with knowledge of the concurrent interrogation of Busch, can be presumed.

That the sole public point of refute for Gregory Greene's involvement in the OCCK killings is that he was reported to have been in jail awaiting trial for the Flint molestations during Timothy King's abduction, but that the records on this are flimsy, is known.

That Detective Lourn Doan of the Southfield Police, a task force member and early supporter of the Busch-Greene relationship to the killings—pushing in that direction as far back as 1977—discovered and noted in 1978 that Greene was indeed not incarcerated during King's abduction but was "out on bond" is generally *not* known but was confirmed by Michigan State Police detective Garry Gray.

All accounts of Christopher Busch's demeanor with friends, family, and coworkers point to his conviviality. He was gentle and friendly with the family housekeeper, his employees at the restaurant in Ess Lake, and even with his victims before fucking them.

Gregory Greene, in contrast, was a loose cannon, hostile and unpredictable. He was born into less fortunate circumstances than Busch and was no doubt envious of Busch's wealth and privilege. He was justifiably bitter at Busch's receiving probation when Greene himself received a sentence of life in prison.

Nobody in the press or police has publicly speculated on the nature of the relationship between Christopher Busch and Gregory Greene. They are called associates, they are called friends, and they are called accomplices in regard to the criminal sexual conduct charges. The mother of a Flint victim believed that Greene and Busch were cousins.

Were they?

REVISION

I'm closing in on what I know is the end. I haven't spoken with my father in two years. I dig out *Wolf in Sheep's Clothing* from a milk crate full of my original research, articles I'd pulled from the Internet before I'd known anything. Published only ten years after the killings stopped, it was as good as it was allowed to be, but I've been privileged with twenty-five more years of cumulative research.

When I reread the preface, I see one good reason why McIntyre's book spins more like an anthem to the police instead of a hard-hitting investigation: The preface states that in 1984, then-retiring Michigan State Police captain Robert H. Robertson approached McIntyre with the idea for the book—not the other way around, with McIntyre seeking out his own subject. Robertson actually edited each chapter for "accuracy of fact and police procedure."

That McIntyre, a well-respected beat writer of the era, appears to have flipped his position from reporter to conduit for police revisionism must be unintentional. I assume that, like the best of journalists, McIntyre fell sway to his sources, the manner of his reporting being less a product of negligence than naïveté at the time, the way a ten-year-old boy gets into a car whose driver he should have either run from or attacked at the scene.

However, I, too, may be a revisionist at heart. Have I not wanted to believe in motivations I've known nothing about? My father's fists swinging into the drywall in those early years, the holes he left behind as detonations in my heart. But what those holes were to him I cannot know; the product of his frustration with the terms of his life, or maybe with his own mother, who I believe hurt him for years with her words?

What, then, will my own children say about me? How will they revise what I have said in these pages after decades have passed? Were there even holes in the walls of my childhood to begin with? Will my own children remember detonations of their own?

Have I hurt my father inordinately by prioritizing my happiness over his anger? My story over his pain? What do I owe his crimes? Discovery? Retribution? How often can the book be written, and rewritten?

MURDER-SUICIDE

With police from cities in both Wayne and Oakland Counties actively involved in the original investigative months of the OCCK, the Michigan State Police was compelled to step in and oversee the proceedings almost from the beginning. While the task force comprised members from multiple jurisdictions, the MSP was boss of the machine, with then lieutenant and soon-to-be captain Robert Robertson as kingpin utilizing his first-in-command, Detective Sergeant Joe Krease, six feet tall and lean but pointedly sturdy, to project manage.

Krease, with the MSP for fourteen years working multiple homicide investigations, was now in charge of the largest manhunt in Michigan history and the largest in the U.S. at the time. Whom they were looking for, Krease couldn't know, but he was a methodical, streetwise cop with an even temper and a pleasant personality that often fooled the unsuspecting. Krease was the cop who would catch you just by sifting through the information and being around.

It's hard to say how much of the information

available to Krease during the OCCK years was pre-sifted and culled before reaching him, but it's important to understand how interwoven Detroit and its environs are. The suburbs might have appeared flashy when compared to the more dismal-seeming streets of Detroit, but the inner-city power structure, the political suits downtown, had far-reaching tentacles. While the MSP ran the business end of the investigation, Detroit was its quiet investor.

Although Richard Lawson, for example, was immediately a person of interest to the task force, it is easy to see how being on the city of Detroit's payroll as an informant might have precluded him from more than cursory inquiry. Like Christopher Busch, another untouchable man, Lawson had been vouched for.

The reach of Detroit was inbred at times. Oakland County's sheriff and undersheriff, Johannes Spreen and John Nichols, respectively, had each been Detroit police commissioners prior to working the OCCK case. Nichols had been commissioner during the 1967 riots that tore the city apart. Spreen began as commissioner a year later, remaining in that capacity until 1970. Both men had cut their teeth on a city in the throes of chaos. With regard to the Oakland County Child Killer case, Spreen and Nichols would have known too much about Detroit to push too deep, against the Lawson lead, against the underbelly of the Cass, against the foundations like the Yondotega Club and its underwriting of the privileged. The two prior police commissioners would have known enough to know less, even when they knew more.

Krease, even with financial resources never before allocated to such a degree for one case, was isolated in his hunt; the long arm of the law was the short end of the stick for Krease, and an apparently good cop's emotional investment in the case went unrequited. That feeling of isolation must have lasted. In 1992, fourteen years after the OCCK Task Force officially shut down, Joe Krease got into an argument with his girlfriend in the parking lot of their apartment complex and shot her through the window of her car as she was trying to drive away.

Neighbors had heard them screaming at one another just prior to that, then watched from their apartment as Krease pulled his gun. The glass on his girlfriend's vehicle shattered, and they knew she'd been killed.

Then Krease put the gun to his own head and pulled the trigger again.

The operations leader of the largest criminal case in Michigan's history went down in a crime of passion, murder-suicide in broad daylight, with witnesses.

I'm out, he must have thought. *I'm getting the fuck out.*

THE PROFILER

In 1977, while the task force was still engaged with its hunt, a national search for criminal profilers beyond the MSP's own experienced detectives began. Dr. Nicholas Groth from the Massachusetts Treatment Center for Sexually Dangerous Persons became a member of the profiling team. The profiler said:

The killer was intelligent but with no formal education.

I think, *Greene.*

The killer was not of a moneyed background or esteemed social standing.

Greene.

The killer was not in a position of authority in the workplace.

Greene.

The killer had a previous record of criminal activity for violence just beneath the degree of violence now being perpetrated by him.

Greene again. Greene, I think.

The profiler said the sex of the child was less relevant to the killer than the age of the child, since the killer's preference was not homo or hetero based but age based in service to the avoidance of confrontation with adult sexuality. This also suggests Greene: Note his belief that he emotionally bonded with the young baseball player he'd molested.

Dr. Groth denoted that the cleansing of the bodies was in service to purification, although I know that the bodies were not cleansed but may have been sloppily wiped down, if that. The haphazardness of any cleaning suggests haste, which certainly can be seen as a rushed cleansing of the act of murder from the killer's conscience. Read Greene in California, hurrying his victim to the hospital after a wave of remorse.

Dr. Groth said that while Mark Stebbins had been struck on the head, no violence other than sexual was inflicted upon his body, suggesting that the strike was unanticipated by the killer and had come only as a reaction in order to subdue. The same can be said about the shotgun blast to Jill Robinson. Think of Greene's striking of the boy's throat in California.

The profiler added the positioning of Mark's and Kristine's bodies to a list of things interpreted as ritualistic. Their final positioning was likely more utilitarian than that, however: They had been shoved into a small trunk for transport, resulting in rigor after several hours of driving. Remember Greene's statements about "driving around with" the unconscious boy in California before dumping him? Timmy's body positioning suggests minimal time in the trunk; Timmy was dumped facedown, suggesting haste. If not for an unknown event that caused the killer to drop Timmy sooner than he'd wished, Timmy would have been positioned more like Mark or Kristine had been. Jill Robinson's shotgun blast to the face, as well as lack of fetal positioning, suggests the possibility that, while initially smothered, she may not have been dead prior to transport and therefore no rigor had set in.

The profiler stated that the killer's "fair" treatment of the children while in captivity suggested his longing for affection and validation. This again calls to mind Greene's statements about seeing himself as a father figure to the boy in California.

What can we assume, then, about why neither city nor county nor state police pursued the Greene leads in light of mounting circumstantial evidence, his admission to hundreds of similar crimes, confessional evidence to his knowledge of at least the Stebbins murder, and a fitting psychological profile?

The only real assumption to make is that competent police from all jurisdictions *did* follow the Greene lead more closely and would have eventually charged him with the OCCK murders if those charges would not have eventually forced them to charge Christopher Busch as well.

It would have been impossible to publicly take down one for the OCCK without taking down the other as a conspirator, as Busch and Greene were virtually joined at the hip in the commission of the crimes.

In short, Greene wasn't charged because Busch was involved.

I AM, TOO

My sister appears on my Facebook wall, commenting on photographs. She tells me she loves me in emailed messages. The syntax is hurried but heartfelt and crisp with affection.

She says, "I am glad you're my brother. I am glad we're talking again."

She's referring to the bounce back from that silence we'd both nurtured well into our thirties, a couple of decades when the pain of our family was too much to triumph over—years that were lean in happiness for her and that had found me cored-out by depression and alcoholism.

She calls me at five a.m. and leaves messages that I can follow, whereas I couldn't years ago, when they were full of desperation instead of the delight of today in them. When I call her back it goes to voice mail, but these days at least I know she'll be listening.

I don't know if she'll be happy forever, but she is happy today, and I can more or less predict that she'll be happy in the immediate tomorrow.

This is my sister thirty-five years ago: her long brown hair running down into legs that build to a spring across our drying lawn in midsummer, her cheeks flushing red in anger, over what I can't remember—over the fury of awakening in a war zone, maybe—the sunlight on her face like a lashing of napalm.

And this is my sister now, thirty-five years later: her voice mails like a hand reaching for my own, saying *Come with me* and *Help me, too,* speaking the language of a girl who would give her brother thirty cents to buy candy, who would beg his forgiveness for a world she couldn't protect him from and didn't herself yet know existed.

When I finally get my sister on the phone, I'm parked outside a coffee shop at the foot of the mountains, and there's snow on the highest peaks and fog beneath them, and after a while she says, "So, did you solve the case?"

My cell phone is hot in my hand, and I am thinking about how fucking young we were so long ago and how everything in my sister's life was still before her and how some of it could still be when I say, "I think so," and then I say, "But maybe it doesn't matter, I guess."

"Yes it does," she tells me.

I can hear her crying over the phone but I think she's maybe smiling through it when she says, "I'm glad I got to see you."

I tell her, "I know you are. I am, too."

WHAT IF THAT FUCKER IS CLEAN?

In August of 1999, some twenty-two years after the killings stopped, Detective Ray Anger traveled to Wyoming to take part in the exhumation of bone, hair, and tissue samples from the grave of David Norberg, the former autoworker from Detroit who'd moved west with his wife and young daughter after being questioned early on about the killings, then died in a car crash in 1981.

Three different tips had come in on Norberg before he moved, based on multiple accusations of sexual advances toward children, but he was cleared of involvement in the OCCK murders after his wife provided multiple alibis. Of lingering interest was Norberg's possession in 1977 of a silver cross with "Kristine" etched into it, although Norberg himself had no publicly known relation to anyone of that name. The necklace, when shown to Mihelich's family, proved not to belong to their Kristine. It was circumstantial, if odd.

Long after his death, Norberg's wife recanted

those earlier alibis and professed her belief that Norberg was the Oakland County Child Killer.

In 1999, Ray Anger and the Oakland County medical examiner traveled to Wyoming, collected Norberg's DNA, and ran it against a pubic hair found on Timothy King. They attempted a mitochondrial match using the same technology that would eventually be used to match the Gunnels and Sloan hairs, although Anger and his representatives left Wyoming without the match they'd been hoping for.

"Now we keep hunting," Anger said to the press. Reflecting on comments he'd reportedly made to Mark Stebbins's mother prior to her death, he added, "I told her, I can't promise I'll ever solve [the case], but I can promise I won't ever stop trying."

I do not know if Ray Anger is among the most sensitive of his brethren in the police or among the most troubling. There remains the possibility that, as relates to the OCCK, Ray Anger is both. It can certainly be said that, just as Christopher Busch remains the fulcrum on the dead end of things, Ray Anger remained at the center of my notes on the living.

I keep coming back to Cathy's texts—*That fucker is dirty*—but what if, at the end of the day, and surprisingly so, Ray Anger is clean?

BUNDLED

In contrast to Gregory Greene's chipped-paint, blue-collar childhood home, the Busch family compound at 3310 Morningview Terrace in Bloomfield Hills was a six-thousand-square-foot, redbrick-and-stone, 1950s-era manor squatting on upwards of an acre of manicured lawn with a sweeping driveway that bisected the lawn and led to a well-kept, columned porch.

On November 20, 1978, the temperature was approximately 30 degrees Fahrenheit at nine a.m., frigid for autumn. The lawn would have been crisped-over and white from the overnight freezing of dew when Charles Busch, the eldest son, arrived with an officer in tow to check on his younger brother after the housekeeper couldn't enter the house.

The officer broke out a window to gain entry. Upstairs in the bedroom where Christopher Busch lay, nothing seemed right. The body was wrapped tightly in a blanket, there was no blood anywhere, and the officer implied that the room felt almost staged, complete with ligatures, shotgun shells of the same caliber used to blow Kristine away, and a pencil drawing of one of the dead boys that'd been missing at first, although he later claimed not to believe in the actual staging theory.

Four hours later, at 1:00 p.m., an autopsy was performed by the Oakland County medical examiner, Dr. Robert Sillery. Christopher Busch's blood-alcohol level was a prodigious 0.41 percent, the result of drinking combined with postmortem fermentation. He had been dead for at least a couple of days, Sillery said. A greater toxicology screen was done, with no indication of poisoning prior to the gunshot wound between his eyes.

By the end of the afternoon, Sillery had labeled Christopher Busch's death a suicide, although— factoring in the minimal evidence obtained by Sillery at the autopsy, the positioning of Busch's body, the lack of residue and blood spatter, and the absence of a suicide note—it would be impossible to reasonably conclude that the reported gunshot wound was self-inflicted.

Two years later, Sillery was investigated by the attorney general's office for providing fraudulent autopsy results in an unrelated case. He was suspected of bribe taking and gross incompetence. He was eventually suspended from practicing medicine.

CHRISTOPHER BUSCH HAD been tucked tightly into his blanket. His hands had no access to the trigger of a rifle held firmly to his fore-head, so he'd either been shot in the head while sleeping like that—shot in the head while either sleeping differently or awake and then bundled up afterward for a failed attempt to transport him (he was heavy!)—or carried into the home postmortem via the garage and dropped onto his bed.

Regardless, Christopher Busch and the circumstantial treasures within his room had been intentionally left for discovery.

At the time of Busch's death, Gregory Greene was already imprisoned and would be serving life. Even if not publicly revealed as the Oakland County Child Killer, Greene would die behind bars and maybe that was good enough for those in the know.

Busch, however, had been a loose end, until his death.

Cathy Broad had been adamant that the PD was stonewalling the families to hide the incompetence of their original investigators, and I'd agreed—but wasn't it possible that they'd been protecting something else completely, maybe having bundled loose ends in their own special way?

Who *did* kill Christopher Busch, after all?

Dirty and clean—in a politically complicated world, sometimes the two can be very much alike.

LITTLE MONSTER

I am accustomed, by now, to losing everything I gain. Even out here in Idaho, I remain a product of Detroit inside, set out to rust beside the river. Through the surrender of fall to winter this year, I have receded into isolation.

But I can no more continue to accept the gradual icing-over of streets in the neighborhood outside my window than I can bear the solitude of my anger, whose winters seem never-ending. The way I will win, if there is victory at all, will not be via a blood fighting of my father, of the crimes against the children of Detroit, of my station in the past—haunting me still—or of even the details in the whitewashing of the OCCK murders, but via, as all truths are pulled from war, the stamina of my compassion on the battlefield.

Or that's what I have been told in therapy, anyway, during the past six court-ordered sessions that have dog-eared the changing of the seasons for me after the beginnings of a custody battle over my son. In therapy, I am told to be cautious of the tendency of a sense of moral superiority to cloud understanding, and to accept that true knowledge exists only through compassion for the imperfect. How this affects my hunt through the OCCK terrain is no doubt as substantially esoteric as engaging with these rules in my personal life.

I wonder if it is possible to embrace the weakest links in the OCCK case—for instance, to love Gregory Greene, to shower compassion upon him as merely another member of the human race maneuvering through the complexities of a world that incubates people like him. Can I accept that these killings may be less the actions of an individual and more the inevitable consequence of a sanctioning society? I do not know the answer to that.

I do know that, regardless of my respect for the human race and sensitivity to societal quirks, if Gregory Greene had been found to have touched one of my children, I'd have put a blade in his neck, and in doing so I would have killed two people at once: the Gregory Greene that had become the monster his adulthood had diagrammed, and the Gregory Greene who had been the small boy lounging in his mother's lap at some point, not yet knowing the beast he would become, and perhaps not in control of that becoming.

ON IMPERFECTIONS

I would like a readership to find fault in perfection, should I threaten to deliver it, the story winding itself down on the streets of Detroit, my hooded figure bookending the tale, or with my hair in the wind riding a ferry through the frigid chop toward the Foxes; for it is only in the imperfections, the unknown aspects of the OCCK, that we are allowed to see the truth: that no serial murder case in the history of modern criminal justice has had so many leads, and for as long a duration, without a single arrest. That we are not allowed to know why has provided us with a certain kind of understanding.

There remain holes in this story, and yet, as in many mysteries, the answer can be found by simply reaching through those holes, the truth only an arm's length away after all.

That a privately sponsored investigation into Adam Starchild's financial statements would detail the listing of a heavily insured, extensive art collection, including works similar to the one missing from the McKinney gallery, is of interest.

That South Fox Island would be found to have

served as a port of transfer for the drug trade, an illicit accompaniment to its pornographic brethren on the northern island, with cocaine swinging in from the southern seas via East Coast hubs—New Jersey and New York—and smut traveling from Michigan toward those same hubs, to be swung out across the Atlantic for the titillation of its European clientele, is also of interest.

That planes go down over frigid waters, automobiles explode, suicides abound, blood is sprayed on dashboards in the parking lots of apartment complexes, lives are gassed in the suburban single-car garages of spring, birth certificates are burned and passports faked, and composite after composite matching suspect after suspect and vehicle after vehicle matching imprint after testimony after composite alike can, without resolution, be overwhelming. It can feel as if all we've been left with is the mystery, even after everything that's been learned about these murders. And yet, the loose ends, flapping like strands of silk, remain just on the other side of an ever-closing hole in the tale:

A single arm, like a magician's disappearing down a hat, can retrieve a bouquet.

SPRING

I noticed flowers growing along the side of my house today. One small blue flower, the shape of a bulbous dime balancing on the thinnest of stems, rising only inches from the dirt, and then several clumps of a larger, .44-caliber-shaped tubular variety of varying colors, everything precariously reaching, not yet fully trusting in the arrival of spring, not yet opening but willing to rise up and peek around in the warmer air.

Today is March 26, 2013, thirty-six years and four days after Timothy King was found shucked from the palm of his neighborhood into a channel along a slender road in the darkest of hours. It will be 57 degrees today, 65 degrees tomorrow.

I do not know the names of the species of wild things, but my father knew them intimately. As a teenager, when I began to see my father once a month or so and witnessed the flowers that had sprung around his home, I could perceive that the Latin and the English held different weights for him. He was aligned with the former: to speak, when naming a species, the words that ended in -*ia* and -*is,* the sounds of a language curling

369

upward or stretching out, instead of the harder consonants in his native language.

His own father, practicing medicine, had spoken in the Latin as well, while his mother reportedly spoke only with a venom that contaminated him from early on. While I recognized my grandmother's knife skills with language, she was warm to the touch, coddling my needs with the smell of her perfume and the largesse of her hair, reddened like evening sunlight across glass.

That my father, feeling the way he did about her, would choose the more marbled aesthetic of formalism represented by my grandfather does not surprise me. My father's seeming lack of genuine affection for his wife and children was either birthed from the short-circuiting of his maternal relationship or from his own silenced traumas, or from that which we as mortals can know little of: the recognition of the timeless and divine in his father, the idolization of the mechanics of the particular. These were the restraints that kept my father from crossing over, that allowed him to function when so much inside of him was raging. Why my displacement of his hairbrush from one side of the sink to the other caused such hostility in him that it terrified me even at nineteen. How I had been learning that anger and love were of the same bloodline. Why I buried myself in the structuring of sentences to escape the threat of that destiny.

I do not know what I feel when I stand in the mirror and study the body that has been marked by my own hand at times. From the moment the first belt across my back became release, it somehow did so in imitation of the dotted bruises from my brother's jersey that were pounded into the flesh when he was a boy. That the two could exist in harmony—the preservation of my brother's pain, which he has not asked of me, and my own exulting—seems a blasphemy upon the gift of life. And yet it was a thing that happened, in a time that requested it, that I must purge by making known.

In the marking is the release, as I have marked my wall with the photo of police officer Reni Lelek, the only clipping from my files that I continue to reflect upon, in order to let her go. Although I have taken no further measures to reach her, I know that in Reni is the image of Ellie, and that in Ellie is the image of my mother in those early years of my clasping to her hand. That I do not come to find Reni Lelek dead or seek her in life is no surprise. She may be, after all, beyond the rendering of her portrait, a mere imagining of that purest of loves, in the moment of its capture, before its striking.

The rendering of my father in these pages may be, unfairly, the mere rendering of my hurt. Although I have told the truth, I have indeed left out those forgotten moments that were perhaps

371

overpowered by my coming of age, the way I must have softly leaned into my father's lap as a toddler or chased what was thrown by him to be retrieved by me: a ball across the carpeted bedroom floor, a single marble across the tiles where the bathtub met the doorjamb.

In my clearest moments I think fondly of my father revisiting my childhood home as I, too, have done, and imagine his car pulled to the curb, his motor idling, his memories of our time spent inside those walls, in greater richness than I have allowed him here, a thing that fills the silence.

WHEN THE WEATHER first warmed last week, I watched my son through the matchbook-sized monitor of my Flip cam, set on a tripod in the driveway; he was captured in a square of light that saw him doing curb slides on his skateboard, the sunshine warping against his leather jacket. At thirteen now, his body is lengthening, the sound of an electric razor comes from the bathroom some nights before he showers, and the scent of cologne lingers in the living room when I've returned from driving him to school.

I know that one day he will be gone from me of his own accord and that within his absence will be my failure to have been perfect for him, in the most difficult times that we faced together, when he needed that perfection from me most. I can hope that within his absence will be his joy as well, and the remnants of his verve, and I can know that he will return.

My daughter's leaving will preface his, only a year from now when she fills her car with the many treasures I've watched her accumulate over the years—her record collection, the boxes of books that went unpacked after the split, her guitars, her amplifier, the magazine photos from her wall—and hopefully with her she will take the confidence to be a woman in a world that I have not changed at all, except via my unflinching adoration of her.

Time will tell how I will be judged by them both. Whether I said the right thing in moments of stress, whether I gave of myself enough during the years of my hunt, whether I, when time allows again, give everything available—they will be able to tell that story better than I.

Just yesterday I stared at the videos of them taken in a grainy light outside the home we all believed in together: each of them sharing a rope swing at midday, each of them holding a sparkler in the darkest night, each of them running across the sunlit grass as it filled in with summer.

And the sounds they made, the sounds were just incredible.

EPILOGUE

There was water gushing down from the mountaintops by May, a heat fog across the sidewalks by June. With nothing more to hunt, I wandered through coffee shops and sometimes thought I saw my father in the glance back from strangers awaiting their morning double-shot Americanos. Every few days my father's hands appeared to carry a plate past me in line, a small bagel balancing on it as precariously as my memory of him, or I'd brush across what appeared to be his thinning arm on my way out to the street-side tables where I watched a month go by like streaming traffic. I'd look up from my coffee and see my father's figure in another bystander out on a corner awaiting the crosswalk light to change, a question mark hooked into his right fist with nothing to strike, nothing to subdue but regret.

My car had died, and I'd borrowed money to buy a truck that cost me as much in gasoline every week as our grocery bill had cost, scraping away at the inner edges of my bank account once our food stamps had run out again. Sometimes

I'd sit in that truck outside my old home and remember things, but other times, when my kids would come out to the driveway of our rented bungalow, we'd shut ourselves inside the doors of that truck together and feel like a family again, even if we had to bullshit ourselves into forgetting the missing pieces.

Some things never come back, not the splinters of a whittled relationship, especially. If you are lucky enough to get a second chance, it often appears in the form of a mutated piece of drift-wood no bigger than the arms that carry it from shore to bed again, all the extra things it used to be now planed away by its passage home.

Kristine Mihelich's birth father, I'll soon learn, will commit suicide, a troubling detail that I receive via text message from Detroit, sent to me across two thousand miles.

Only a few months after Kristine's father passes, Ray Anger will die, too, having sustained a head injury due to a fall in his home. In the hospital I was born in, just outside of Detroit proper, Ray Anger languished for a month after his fall, I am told, then passed.

The daughter and the nephew of the cop named Flynn will begin a correspondence with me via email shortly after Anger's death, and we'll eventually have long phone calls wherein the silences between our conviviality and shared knowledge are not awkward, only ruminative with the distance of decades we can no longer get back but, with grace, can move forward from.

And Vincent Gunnels, I'll learn soon after, will be back in prison after a drug-related probation violation.

The city of Detroit, however, still crippled by bankruptcy during the periods of my visiting, will turn a corner toward something cleaner and brighter on the horizon. Millions of dollars in investment capital, mostly in the technology sector, will turn many of the once-rotted-out downtown high-rises into hives of millennial-inspired productivity. And from the center of the city outward, moneyed hipsters, street-savvy artists, and blue-collar industrialists will carve out the smaller nooks, renovating cinder-block storage spaces into corner shops and restaurants, things bustling and hot again, Detroiters moving ahead in the ways they'd been taught to by their history, with brick and mortar and fists, and with hustle.

THE LAST WEEKEND in June, I walked into a church downtown and bent my knees, holding on to the wooden shoulder of a pew. I'd expected to cry but couldn't. There was sunlight coming through the rear windows behind me, and after a while I could feel a heat on the back of my neck. I thought of my father sitting across a table from me in a diner before our food had come, the smell of Old Spice freshly splashed against the carriage of his jaw in reminder that I would always be younger than him, always subservient to what was greater and stronger than what I could control. It is why I haven't told my father's story in its entirety within these pages, why I have left out pieces that were not mine to tell, those pieces that remain ellipses when one asks, "Whatever did he do that was just so bad?"

I have been anointed, by the liquor of his memory and the sheer, overwhelming largesse of faith, in spite of my instinct to kill.

By midsummer I was working full-time as a fraud investigator for the medical insurance industry, conducting surveillance on worker's compensation claimants, diagramming and photographing accident scenes, red-flagging exorbitant injury claims, and recommending cases for prosecution. It was a solid paycheck for the first time in many years, and I became good at it. Sometimes out on surveillance, when there was nothing but myself and the long hours encased in the blackout glass of my vehicle, is when I felt most at home. I was a figurine inside a snow globe of the slightly shaken quiet of whatever years remained for me. It's how my brother must have felt entombed in a Humvee during his mission sets; how my sister may have uncomfortably felt in the wraparound blur of my uncle's prurient gaze; how my mother all those years ago must have felt in the vacuum of our home, her eyelids fluttering to a crease against the thickening glass that separated our family from the roving world.

I worry sometimes about the pruning of my children from my father's grasp. By dragging them to safety, I know that I have cheated them of the bits of joy he may have offered, in time, when patience allowed. I worry equally that, in tearing myself away from his will, I have torn through the fabric of our family's story too violently and, in the course of our lives, it might be proven, irreparably. Neither the authority of my god, the wielding of morality, or even the heartbeat of a decent instinct guided me with grace; I raged, I raged and lashed against the passing of my nights, and in the faces of strangers I see my father's impunity overwhelmed by the immeasurable hurt I imagine to have caused him during what are undoubtedly his final years of life. I have always wanted my father's love, but today, now, I want his forgiveness, too.

TWO WEEKS AGO it snowed for days and by Christmas Eve our small city was perfectly painted for the holiday season: white on the lawns, with glowing twirls of color up the banisters, lining the eaves, and framing the upstairs windows of the tidiest homes.

I drove, my children in the backseat and, beside

378

me and across the armrest, a woman I would come to love so dearly for the many years ahead, her hand reaching for my knee and resting there softly as the snowed-over subdivision streets unfolded in my headlamps. We gazed at the twinkling lights to either side of us, the Christmas trees in the big downstairs windows of the homes hung with candy and tinsel. For the first time in years I didn't notice the inversion that must have also painted the world in front of me. There must have been a darkness somewhere, but I didn't feel it. I only saw the lights shining through.

It had taken so long, but the peace my mother had wanted for us all those winters ago—with my stocking-capped forehead pressed to the rear window of her station wagon as we cruised those neighborhoods where happiness seemed to live, my index finger tracing through the fogged-over glass and wondering how many years, how many years it would be—had possibly come.

ACKNOWLEDGMENTS

S ome had faith enough for the both of us, and I thank you for that. To the family members of the victims, your sacrifice should never have been. I am with you in spirit, always. David Klein, your years of encouragement were often all that pulled me from the floor at night. My dear friends, Ori Lev and John McMillian, I thank you as well, for the decades of kinship and phone calls that have been my lifeline. Dani, this could not have been accomplished without your enormous heart and loving years of brilliant company, which I will endlessly want more of. Adilyne Elizabeth and Jackson Sugar, who will forever be my northern stars, I steer toward you always. And to so many others along the way: Victoria, it too often goes without saying but we did a really good thing for a very long time; my incredibly reliable and dedicated first responders, Jon Keller and Tyler McMahon; Ben LeRoy, for saying yes when everything was looking like no; Kate, Chelsea, Molly, and Elisa for making this so much better; the *Homeland* writers, for their early and wonderful support; my longtime cheerleader, friend, and inspiration, Adam Acey; little Jenny Forgache, my first love, sanctuary, friend, and, in some ways, the center of this tale; Dylan Bruno, for instructing me on the circular nature of existence; Michael Hoffman, force of nature and companion in a time that mattered; Tom, whose rides home in his Cadillac offered much-needed respite; Jill, Michael, and Jodi for the road trips and sanctuary; my mother, unsung hero of the story then and now; David Yasuda, for the lunches and the caring; Sarah Masterson, for always texting at the very right time; Emily Skopov, Sandra Andersen, Al Greenberg, and Janet Holmes; the 208 Kickstarter backers, including Thomas Obrey, Amy Shuler, C.W.W., and Margaret and Bob Church; Shannon from back in the day; Michael, Elissa, and Max; and Barry, Cathy, Chris, Erica, and Tom, for your vulnerability, access, records, and embrace of this project. And for my father, who, regardless of the tale herein, deserves some respect for having been, off and on, present in the ways that he knew how to be. I am especially thankful, as well, to the Idaho Commission on the Arts and the National Endowment for the Arts for their financial support along the way. May we, together, rise above these difficult times.

Books are produced in the United States using U.S.-based materials

Books are printed using a revolutionary new process called THINKtech™ that lowers energy usage by 70% and increases overall quality

Books are durable and flexible because of Smyth-sewing

Paper is sourced using environmentally responsible foresting methods and the paper is acid-free

Center Point Large Print
600 Brooks Road / PO Box 1
Thorndike, ME 04986-0001 USA

(207) 568-3717

US & Canada:
1 800 929-9108
www.centerpointlargeprint.com